IN OUR
SHOES

IN OUR SHOES

ON BEING A YOUNG BLACK WOMAN IN NOT-SO "POST-RACIAL" AMERICA

BRIANNA HOLT

PLUME

PLUME

An imprint of Penguin Random House LLC
penguinrandomhouse.com

LIBRARY OF CONGRESS CATALOGING-IN-PUBLICATION DATA

Names: Holt, Brianna, 1995– author.
Title: In our shoes: on being a young Black woman in not-so
"post-racial" America / Brianna Holt.
Description: [New York, New York] : Plume, [2023] |
Includes bibliographical references.
Identifiers: LCCN 2022052483 (print) | LCCN 2022052484 (ebook) |
ISBN 9780593186398 (paperback) | ISBN 9780593186404 (ebook)
Subjects: LCSH: African American young women—Social conditions. |
African American women—Social conditions. | African Americans—Social
conditions. | Stereotypes (Social psychology)—United States. |
Holt, Brianna, 1995– | African American young women—Biography. |
United States—Race relations.
Classification: LCC E185.86 .H6955 2023 (print) | LCC E185.86 (ebook) |
DDC 305.48/896073 [B]—dc23/eng/20221123
LC record available at https://lccn.loc.gov/2022052483
LC ebook record available at https://lccn.loc.gov/2022052484

Printed in the United States of America

1st Printing

BOOK DESIGN BY LORIE PAGNOZZI

*For teenage Brianna, who struggled
so much with self-love, confidence,
and opening up to others.
Look at you now.*

CONTENTS

IN OUR SHOES

INTRODUCTION

Most authors reserve the introduction of their book as an opportunity to explain who they are or describe what led them to writing their book. For this book specifically, I find it most important to first use this section as a disclaimer to my readers and a reminder that the experiences and views expressed throughout these nearly three hundred pages are my own and those of the women I interviewed. The beauty in being a Black woman is the complexity and diversity we have within our own race. We vary in skin tones, hair textures, and features. We also vary in upbringing, ethnicities, and nationalities. Some of us have two Black parents, some of us have one. All this diversity allows for variety in walks of life, privileges, and setbacks. In this part memoir, part cultural critique, I have done my best to describe what it means to be a young Black woman navigating "post-racial" America through my memories, recollections, and experiences. I'd also like to acknowledge that *diversity* is a term that does, of course, encompass so many groups and communities, such as religious background, sexual orientation, gender identity, and people with disabilities, which I do not focus on in this book. All of this to say, not everyone will share the same experiences as I have written about them, and for that reason, I ask you, dear reader, to read between the lines just as much as the lines themselves. There have been several occasions when I have been nervous and worried about writing this book because of the vulnerability I've had to take on to share memories that I've spent the greater part of my life trying to bury. I hope that you will be open-minded and nonjudgmental about the experiences I've chosen to share with the world, which I did not create for myself. What I've learned most about being a woman during this era, but more specifically a Black woman, when people are free to share their opinions online, sometimes with anonymity, is that when Black women advocate for their well-being, share the harm others have caused them, or even express their joy, it is oftentimes met with scrutiny. In this book, I've done just that.

When I was young kid, I enjoyed journaling in my diary and writing fictionalized stories about my life, but I never imagined myself writing a book. At least not nonfiction. Surely not a collection of essays. As a trending news journalist, the thought of having any deadline longer than a week gave me immense anxiety. Plus, I always imagined authors and novelists to be the best of the best when it came to writing, or people who had something so thought-provoking to contribute to society that it should be documented forever, not just on the internet, where things could be forgotten, removed, archived. Surely, I thought, contributing to the literary world was never in the cards for me. Until it was.

The summer of 2020 was a time of many societal and cultural changes—COVID-19 was at its peak, the great exodus led many people to leave their jobs in the midst of economic uncertainty, several millennials moved back in with their parents, and a racial reckoning consumed both social media and the streets. Like several of my peers, I grew restless from having my social life stolen from me as I temporarily left my apartment in New York City to camp out at my childhood home and reverted to a lifestyle I hadn't experienced since high school. Each day merged into the next as I woke up just minutes before 9 a.m., logged onto my work laptop from my bed, and edited articles about viral TikTok videos and celebrity fashion trends for a publication that was underpaying and overworking me. In the evening, I'd watch a movie with my mom and scroll through photos of protests on my Instagram feed, feeling an intense urge to join others outside. But, as someone who is immunocompromised, and living with my mother at the time, I couldn't afford to risk contracting COVID by protesting in crowds during the height of a global pandemic. At that point, there was no vaccine and very little understanding of how life-threatening the disease was. So instead, I started to focus my freelance writing on race, identity, and news surrounding the reemergence of the Black Lives Matter movement. As I read through studies on topics like adultification bias and chatted with sources about their experiences with microaggressions, I'd read my drafts aloud to my mother before sending them off to my editor. It was during these bonding moments that I started to realize my mother didn't fully grasp what I was writing about. Having grown up during the mid-'50s, she was not familiar with these terms or their impact. She hadn't heard of phrases like *unconscious biases*, *virtue signaling*, or *cultural appropriation*. *Blaccent* and *blackfishing* had not yet been introduced into her vocabulary. When I explained these terms in detail, she was quick to understand their meanings but hadn't grown up with the same language or open dialogue that growing up with the internet provided me. During my mother's youth, receiving information about civil rights movements often involved attending meetings, joining organizations, or walking in a march. But for millennials, who grew up during the rise of social media platforms, becoming aware, or as some would say, woke, is accessible every day, online, where communities of thousands of people can share their experiences, their research, and their wisdom, in seconds.

More importantly, in these conversations with my mother, I started to realize that a lot of the obstacles and challenges young Black women of my generation are dismantling and combating are not widely known, not even to our own parents. If my Black mother wasn't aware of the word *misogynoir* or the ways in which colorism negatively impacts young dark-skinned girls and women of today, then how could she support me as I faced the obstacles thrown at me daily? Or why would

I expect men and women of other racial backgrounds to also have this knowledge? If there is not widespread education or media focus on the often silent, persisting issues young Black women face today, then how could a society ever begin to support young Black women? If some of the older Black women who raised me are still unknowingly enforcing respectability politics, if some of the Black men in my family continue to spread colorist ideology, if some of my white colleagues aren't aware of the ways they uphold racist stereotypes about Black women in the workplace, and if some of my non-Black peers aren't knowledgeable about the ways in which white supremacy influences them to look down upon Black women, then how do we begin to move closer to creating better conditions for Black women? In chatting with my mother, and later her friends, I realized that the niche issues negatively impacting the livelihood of young Black women in my generation are almost completely unknown, mostly because there is a collective belief—a false one—that we are living in a post-racial society.

How can a society truly be post-racial when there was so much collective surprise over events like the murders of George Floyd, Ahmaud Arbery, and Breonna Taylor? When many people, including people in my own circle, reacted with shock as two thousand rioters stormed the Capitol without the National Guard being called? When Kyle Rittenhouse's not-guilty sentence was greeted by so many with confusion over how he could not only be decriminalized, but also painted simultaneously as a victim and a hero? For me and so many of my Black friends, none of these events were surprising. When you're conscious and aware that racism hasn't necessarily lessened, but instead disguised itself systematically, these events are to be expected in "post-racial" America.

Because of triumphs like the first Black president, the first Black vice president, and Black women winning Oscars, even my own my mother, like many Americans, was somewhat convinced that we are living in a post-racial era. From a young Black poet reading at the 2021 presidential inauguration to a rise in interracial partnerships, there is a clouded image of America as a rehabilitated nation of unity that welcomes and celebrates a diverse society. The greatest gymnast is a young Black woman (Simone Biles), the biggest pop star is a young Black woman (Beyoncé), the most exceptional tennis player in the world is a young Black woman (Serena Williams), the most popular young actress in Hollywood is a Black woman (Zendaya), and any hip-hop fan will likely tell you that their favorite female rapper is a young Black woman. With so many young Black women dominating culture, entertainment, sports, and politics, it becomes difficult for a society to grapple with the fact that young Black women are still most in need of support and advocacy.

While millennial Black women may not be dealing with the same blatant racism that earlier generations endured, it would be fallacious to presume that conditions have improved. Instead, they've modernized to fit the inconspicuously racist era created by the digital age and somewhat progressive politics, but the parallels make it hard for most people to recognize. While the women before us fought to integrate into schools, Black millennial women are the most educated demographic of women in America. And while Black women of the Gen X and baby boomer generations experienced an era without the right to vote, we grew up with a Black first lady and first Black woman vice president in the White House. I understand why it's difficult to imagine that young Black women are falling behind our peers, and simple to dismiss our complaints by tying them to our generation's characterizations of laziness and dissatisfaction. But the only thing that's changed for Black millennial women is opportunity. Opportunity not necessarily made possible by a societal shift in how young Black women are accepted, but more so the opportunity created by our own activism and demand, and a widespread ideology of showing up unapologetically Black. We have a tool that previous generations did not—the internet. Through social media we are able to share our thoughts and experiences with the masses, create consequences for those who discriminate against us, and build communities of powerful women who are challenging the status quo. We can easily access studies and think pieces that provide us with literature, knowledge, and wisdom that our education systems withheld from us. In many ways, the internet provides us with a platform that society has so long tried to withhold from us.

At other times, however, the internet has also been our greatest opponent. In many ways, it distorts our presentation. Whenever we do something and post it online, the world gets to share its negative opinion. Non-Black people and women often mimic our behavior and grow in popularity from their modern-day minstrel TikTok videos of them cosplaying in our expression. Online, Black women are reduced to clichés through non-Black people's excessive use of GIFs, reaction videos, voice-overs, and songs featuring Black women. In many ways, social media has become an incentive to perpetuate racist stereotypes that fuel the hypersexualization of Black girls and the justification of violence against Black women. These innocent yet harmful portrayals of Black women online and in the media result in reduced outrage when Black girls and women are assaulted or killed.

The lack of control Black women hold in how we are perceived online, in the media, and during our encounters with others is what keeps century-old stereotypes relevant. It is what we have in common with our predecessors—a lack of autonomy in how we are perceived by anyone who is not us. Oftentimes, young Black women are categorized as angry, sassy, sexual, and strong—which we sometimes are, as women of all different backgrounds are, but not in the way white culture assumes or portrays us. A lot of young Black women actually *are* angry. We have many things to be angry about. We are four times more likely to die during childbirth than white women. Nearly 34 percent of missing girls and women are Black, despite making up only 15 percent of the U.S. female population. One in four Black women will be sexually assaulted before the age of eighteen, one in five Black women are survivors of rape, 40–60 percent of Black women report being subjected to coercive sexual contact by age eighteen, and 40 percent of sex-trafficking survivors in the United States are Black women. Due to negligence and systemic racism in healthcare settings, we are more likely to live with diabetes, obesity, high blood pressure, and major depression and have double the risk for stroke. We are paid 64 percent of what non-Hispanic white men are paid. We are the least likely women to be contacted on dating apps. We quite literally create the language and culture of our generation yet rarely reap the benefits. And during this pandemic, we are more likely to be jobless and die from COVID-19. Of course Black women are angry; who wouldn't be? But what we are more angry about is that our conditions are not improving. We are angry about being angry about the same things we saw our mothers and grandmothers being angry about. We are angry about the delusion of many of our allies in believing that "things are better" for us now just because issues are less blatant or because our allies are ignorant to the issues that exist. We are angry that in the twenty-first century we still have to advocate for our basic human rights, and that no one seems to see our battles because there continue to be so many "first Black woman to..." victories. We are angry, but not for the reasons the media has concluded. In fact, the media never asks the angry Black woman what she is actually angry about.

When I first watched Malcolm X's famous 1962 "Who Taught You to Hate Yourself?" speech on YouTube, when working on the proposal for this book, one line made sense of the anger I had been feeling as a young Black woman. "The most disrespected person in America is the Black woman. The most unprotected person in America is the Black woman. The most neglected person in America is the Black woman." In this decade, Malcolm's words still run deep but are camouflaged by the way society pulls from, imitates, and capitalizes on millennial Black womanhood. While Black women of previous generations were often denied access to white establishments, schools, and businesses, young Black women today are dealing with the unconscious biases and microaggressions that have resulted from our being allowed in these white establishments, which were never created with the vision of including us. Black women of previous generations were taught to assimilate, fit in, and shrink their Blackness. Young Black women today are toiling between the lines of being unapologetic about their expression, on the one hand, and, on the other, knowing that unconscious biases toward their expression can decrease employment opportunities, change how they're treated in medical settings, and have a negative impact on their social outcomes. Black women of previous generations were subjected to discrimination blatantly, from comfortable racists, while young Black women are navigating subtle racism from people who self-proclaim to be woke allies. Older Black women experienced racist encounters when they left the comfort of their homes; young Black women are subjected to racism even at home, every time they get online. For young Black women, the digital age provides us with no escape from traumatic news, racist comments and posts, and frequent reminders that the world does not take us seriously.

In being connected online, we are creating more autonomy for our cohort. Together, we're unlearning our own trauma, passed down to us by our mothers and grandmothers, who were raised under respectability politics and white professionalism in order to create better conditions for the next generation of Black women. We've begun to reject the ideals that helped them survive in a less connected world, like relaxing their hair to integrate into society or code-switching in the office to move up the corporate ladder. These differences between young Black women and older Black women sometimes result in disapproval and misunderstanding of our behavior and our demands, but I have faith that the women before us can recognize that we are not rejecting their advice and teachings, but rejecting abiding by the same white judgment and unspoken rules that didn't allow them to be their full selves. We are choosing not to believe that our natural hair is unmanageable, that our skin is too dark (whatever that means), that our laugh is too loud, or that the way we dress makes us "fast." We are not allowing every part of our being to be picked apart, criticized, and judged by anyone but ourselves. We are not ignoring our stress and we are removing ourselves from relationships and establishments that do not value us as humans. Yet still, in many ways, young Black women and Black women of previous generations are dealing with the same issues—which is why young Black women are unwilling to settle for our current conditions. We have a reference point—the struggles and obstacles of our foremothers—to compare our predicaments with. We have not changed positions on the social hierarchy. We continue to be a highly underpaid demographic, receive inadequate healthcare, and have a higher mortality than our non-Black female counterparts. Black women offer emotional support and advocate for other communities and groups but are left to fend for themselves. Black women are dying at exponential rates—from COVID, from childbirth, from medical neglect and physical abuse—but breathe life into society with all that they offer. Imagine a world without Black women, without Black women's contributions, and if that imagined world seems at all boring, bland, or regressed, then maybe this book will enlighten you, dear reader, to step up and show up for Black women.

With all this information out in the open, and how obvious it is that our contributions are instrumental, I've asked myself, how is it that our issues go seemingly unaddressed? What I've sometimes found, when talking with white folks, other women of color, and Black men, is that it's easier for a person to claim they are against an issue than to become self-aware about how they give rise to an issue. But there is no true value in publicly stating you are against the mistreatment of young Black women without then offering ways to support them. Especially when your understanding of Black women does not come from having close friends or romantic partners who are Black, but through parasocial interactions and media consumption, it creates a psychological disconnect where people believe they are progressive and informed about another group of people without any profound relationships or interactions in real life to base this on. Most non-Black women look up to some prominent Black woman celebrity. Whether they idolize Beyoncé or Zendaya, binge shows like *Insecure*, or own a copy of Michelle Obama's *Becoming*, most of them believe that their relationship with Black women—which mostly exists through film, music, and social media consumption—is healthy and approved by Black women. As if being a fan of someone who is a star is equal to supporting Black women in real life. Many white people's relationship with Black people is not firsthand or substantial, not empathetic or personable, but exists merely through entertainment or being online. It creates a manipulated and faulty understanding of a group of people who are not present in their social circles, schools, or workplaces. It consists of exclusive admiration and support, from a distance, that isn't afforded to the entire group but only to those who have reached a high social status. If our society would place worth on and support Black women without the requirement of those women being extraordinary, then maybe we'd see a shift in the conditions of ordinary Black women.

Just as dangerous as these parasocial relationships is the language used to describe the mistreatment that Black women are subjected to. When I first wrote about the fact that Black women face a higher risk of pregnancy complications, the weight of simple unconscious biases became apparent to me. Actually, unconscious biases, or any biases, for that matter, are not simple at all. Yet our society has developed a language that reduces and waters down words and facts surrounding Black harm, causing outsiders to believe we are closer to dismantling racism than we actually are. Essentially, the way we overstate national progress toward racial justice minimizes the trials at play. When white people believe they are not racist but admit to holding some unconscious biases, it creates this false idea of being in the home stretch in self-work. If an unconscious bias, like perceiving Black women as strong, then furthers the idea that Black women can endure more stress and pain than other women, then causes people to think Black women have the ability to power through in times of need, which results in Black women being neglected in healthcare settings, causing Black women to face a higher risk of pregnancy complications—you're very far from being at the finish line of self-work. The same goes for language surrounding microaggressions. All microaggressions are irritating, and when combined, so that Black women are constantly being subjected to microaggressions, they have proven to increase hypertension, cardiovascular disease, diabetes, and respiratory conditions in Black women. So how micro is an aggression that can alter your health and well-being? Not micro at all.

To many people, acts of white supremacy are defined as blatant racism, like a mass shooter attacking a Black church, or systemic racism, like voter suppression in Black neighborhoods, but white supremacy begins with biases that started as thoughts and then transcended that to become real-life repercussions. In a racist world, what so many self-proclaimed progressive people seem to misunderstand is that unconscious biases allow white supremacy to thrive. Therefore, it is the social responsibility of non-Black people, but mostly white and white-passing people, to make thoughtful choices about the media that they project onto the world, how they interact with Black women, and in what ways they can right the wrongs of their history to create better conditions for Black women. In fact, the majority of the obstacles young Black women face come at the hands of others. At first mention, that might sound like a dramatic generalization, but Black women do not wield power in politics, in lawmaking, in healthcare, in media, or in any of the other institutions that so often neglect us. It is the responsibility of our allies, of Black men, and especially of white people to use their respective privileges to protect and do right by us. So, with this book, I hope to provide a look into our lives, so that you, dear reader, can begin to understand us, and the relationship you hold with us.

CHAPTER 1

It's Different in My Body

I started working on the proposal for this book when I was twenty-five, and then writing the book itself when I was twenty-six. The material has been in development since 1994—seven months before my birth, when my mother attended her first prenatal visit upon finding out she was pregnant with me at forty-three. Because of her mature age, family and friends frequently questioned her about her health. Doctors warned her about the risk she was taking by getting pregnant just years before menopause was expected. She was told her chances of complications like high blood pressure and preeclampsia were increased. It was likely that I could be born with Down syndrome and even more likely that my mother would need a C-section. Only the latter took place, and I was prematurely cut from my mother's belly a month before my due date. Age-related risks aside, the chances that my mother would have endured complications throughout the course of her pregnancy were much higher than those of her white counterparts, and her likelihood of dying from pregnancy-related complications was three to four times more likely. These alarming stats suggest that even before I was born, simply by coming from a Black woman, it was pre-determined that my life mattered less.

Disappointingly, the troubles that affected my mother almost thirty years ago are currently affecting Black millennial and Gen Z women today. Just five years before I was born, Black women in 1990 had a 3.3 times greater chance of dying from pregnancy-related complications than white women. Today, Black women are still three to four times more likely to die from a pregnancy-related complication than white women. Despite medical advancements in pregnancy and childbirth, we are the demographic whose conditions have improved the least. Compared to white women, the maternal mortality ratio for Black women was 2.4 times greater in 1940, 3.6 times greater in 1950, 4.1 times greater in 1960, 3.9 times greater in 1970, 3.4 times greater in 1980, and 3.3 times greater in 1990. In 2020, the maternal mortality rate for Black women was 55.3 deaths per 100,000 live births, 2.9 times the rate for white women (19.1) and 3 times the rate for Hispanic women (18.2). Even prominent Black women, with access to the best doctors and medical facilities, are unable to dodge the harms of racial and implicit bias in medicine. Both Beyoncé and Serena Williams have been vocal about how childbirth almost cost them their lives, respectively pointing to our increased risk of preeclampsia and potential neglect by healthcare staff. But it wasn't so much the horror stories of

Black celebrities that solidified, for me, that America doesn't care about Black mothers or their children, as it was the opinions of people in power.

During a *Politico* interview with Senator Bill Cassidy, the response to a question regarding Louisiana's high rates of women dying in childbirth confirmed that regard for Black women is nonexistent. "About a third of our population is African American," he said. "African Americans have a higher incidence of maternal mortality. So, if you correct our population for race, we're not as much of an outlier as it'd otherwise appear. Now I say that not to minimize the issue but to focus the issue as to where it would be." The quote, which aired publicly, was all at once disturbing and yet crystallizing for me.

My grandfather and his family are from Louisiana, and I instantly thought of my female cousins who live there and have to reckon with this sort of disregard for their lives. Because a third of Louisiana's population is Black, there isn't a minor outlier to "correct for." But to say the state doesn't have a problem if a third of that population is removed from the pool, a third of which is Black, suggests the ludicrous and racist ideology of several people who have the power to alleviate this crisis but have failed to do so since my own birth.

I sat across from my mom two summers ago, my baby album in her hands, as she painted a picture of the days leading up to February 21 in 1995. It wasn't the uncertainty she felt that startled me the most but, instead, the doctor's sentiments in response to her concerns at the time. "Whenever I sought reassurance from the doctor about the delicacy of this pregnancy, he'd tell me, 'Don't worry, Black female babies always make it, they are very strong.' You were still in my stomach. Can you believe those were his words of encouragement?" my mother said. It was with that line of advice that she let go of her fears, holding on to that notion for the remainder of her pregnancy. She explained that her doctor was adamant about it, often reiterating that he always witnessed the most strength with Black female babies. It's hard to say whether he had decided against telling my mother, too, that she is a strong Black woman because she is of lighter complexion, with hazel eyes and soft curls—she isn't exactly the visibly presenting Black woman who is typically associated with strength. But her child, me—the daughter of a dark-skinned Black man, who was also attending doctor's visits with my mom—was instantly perceived as a strong Black baby. Trusting authority, my mother would even pass along the belief as an assuring rebuttal to anyone who would comment on her age as a risk factor and remind people that the survival rate was much higher for preemie Black female babies. She didn't have access to a worldwide web of thousands of voices that called out the "strong Black woman" stereotype, and so, ignorantly, like many people of the boomer generation, my mother didn't find a problem with this label, owing to the lack of knowledge at the time. I don't know too many young Black women who would accept that same opinion from a doctor today.

It comes as no surprise that the doctor's claim is not backed by science. Nor is it surprising that a non-Black doctor would place a characteristic like "strength" on an unborn child, especially a Black female child. But this belief, that Black women and girls exude strength, doesn't necessarily stem from a place of endearment or high regard.

Like so many of the other labels placed upon us, our so-called strength dates back to 1619, when slavery was established in the United States. It was believed that Black women could handle emotional and physical stress in ways that other women could not because of the harsh conditions white people subjected their slaves to. By working on plantations, all while enduring physical, emotional, and sexual abuse, and being fed the worst food and given inadequate healthcare, Black women were forced into the role of superhumans with a high pain threshold. As the University of Virginia's Seanna Leath found in her studies about harm associated with the expectation of strength in Black women and girls, Black women are often described as superwomen and our bodies are, often unconsciously, viewed as superhuman. Leath writes,

> This is typically meant as a compliment and received positively when compared to other, blatantly negative stereotypes about Black women that cast them as sexually aggressive, lazy, loud, and ghetto. In my research interviews with young Black women, I find that many consider strength a birthright of Black womanhood. They view their survival amidst the legacies of slavery, colonialism, and

disenfranchisement as a testament to the strength of Black women in U.S. society.

Additionally, a 2016 study of 222 white medical students in the *Proceedings of the National Academy of Sciences* found that half the participants believed Black patients feel less pain than white patients, a medical myth that dates back to medical experiments by white doctors on enslaved Black people in the 1820s. Even in 2021, this myth continues to be perpetuated by medical doctors and workers in healthcare and plays out in the lower quality of healthcare that Black people receive in comparison to their white counterparts. According to the American Bar Association, Black patients are discharged earlier from the hospital than white patients, after surgery—at a stage when discharge can be dangerous or risky; Black patients are more likely to receive less desirable treatments for illness; and Black patients suffering from bipolar disorder are more likely to be prescribed antipsychotics despite evidence that these medications have long-term negative effects and do not produce effective results. In fact, a study observing four hundred hospitals across the United States revealed that Black patients with heart disease received cheaper and older treatments than their white counterparts. More specifically to Black women, they are less likely than white women to receive radiation therapy in conjunction with a mastectomy. Actually, they are less likely to receive mastectomies at all.

So, when my mother's Middle Eastern doctor predicted I

wouldn't die in the womb because "Black female babies are the strongest babies," he assumed that my mother, too, would be fine. Despite her age, despite her child being premature, her doctor believed my Blackness defied the odds. This expectation of strength has worked its way into every aspect of my life. Whether it be my non-Black friends and peers comforting me with "you're so strong" during times of turmoil or my own family members encouraging me to "push through" impossible situations that warrant rest, I've always been expected to be okay and deal with whatever unfair obstacles are thrown my way. It's safe to assume that the majority of these absurd expectations exist for me largely because I am in a Black woman's body.

As I've transitioned from a dependent, sheltered child raised in the South to an independent adult living and working in New York City, it's become ever so evident that strength is not the only attribute associated with existing in a Black, dark-skinned, woman's body. All at once my body, my presence, is intimidating and sometimes perceived as unapproachable to non-Black people, while also undeniably beautiful and often imitated. Other times it means moving between the lines of invisible and hypervisible.

As a teen, being invisible and hypervisible became particularly apparent to me through the reactions of non-Black parents and authority figures. During awards ceremonies, sporting events, and various outings with my white friends, I saw how my Blackness brought people to suspect negative things about my character, my intentions, and my intelligence. I once remember the disbelief and discontent expressed on the faces of white parents at a scholarship ceremony when I was awarded the largest grant. The award was preceded by a lengthy application process, extensive in-person interviews with board members, and multiple long-form essays. Whether these parents were just upset that their child didn't get the award, or they believed I wasn't deserving of the award, I'll never know. But the frequency of these negative reactions and total shock at my achievements by white parents makes me think the latter. At tennis tournaments, white parents would blow up in smoke when their daughters lost to me and would ask them, "How did you let her beat you?" When I announced to the family of one of my close friends, who was white, that I got into the University of Texas, instead of congratulating me, my friend's mom responded, "Really? I wonder why Jess didn't get in, then." At an early age, I realized my hard work, which involved making good grades, long hours of practicing tennis, and joining numerous extracurriculars to prepare myself for future opportunities, had been invisible to some of the white people around me, because they still met my achievements with disbelief and bias.

This kind of bias didn't stop at school. When shopping with a white friend at the mall, I saw how my Blackness cast me as "the friend," the one next to the girl deemed deserving of phenomenal customer service. Anytime my friend and I visited the mall, I longed to be approached by a salesperson at one of the many booths to ask if they could style my hair for free or offer me a perfume sample. When we'd walk into Abercrombie, the sales associates would eagerly try to recruit my friend for a job while I'd stand there trying to figure out what it was about her that was so gravitational. Rarely would they glance in my direction or acknowledge my existence as I stood beside her. But that all changed when we lingered in a store. Oftentimes, the longer we stayed in a store and browsed through the aisles, the more all eyes were suddenly on me. Inexplicably, the store associates would glance over from their registers to make sure I wasn't slipping anything into my bag. We'd make eye contact frequently in the mirrors tacked on the ceiling. In some cases, someone would approach me multiple times to ask if I needed help finding anything, reminding me that I was being watched and that I was expected to do something criminal. This transition, from being invisible to hypervisible, was confusing, especially since middle school was the first time I started to become aware of it. Such innocence and little life experience didn't provide me with an explanation for why this was happening, but I was always aware of feeling othered, or different from my white friends. One specific instance made it immensely clear that these parallels existed solely because I was a Black girl.

During what was supposed to be a casual outing to the mall, I became aware that my problems didn't exist because of my skin but because of *other* people's reactions to it. To me and my community, Black skin was never criminal. I had been surrounded by harmless Black children my entire life. The idea that something was wrong with my skin is one I was made to believe as I entered non-Black spaces and had encounters with non-Black people. One afternoon, my friend's mom dropped the two of us off at the mall, now that we were old enough to be trusted on our own. I specifically remember my friend having more than a hundred dollars to spend, while I had to make do with the fifteen dollars my mom gave me for food. We did our rounds at the mall until we ended up at Forever 21. I noticed my friend slipping cheap jewelry into her purse, with such ease and very little hesitation. But I minded my business. Like most young kids, I felt calling out someone else's bad behavior would only create awkwardness between us. I just knew I had no plans to follow along. My parents would never let me step foot in a mall again without their supervision if I were to steal and embarrass them in such a way.

When my friend suggested I take something too, and pointed out how easy it would be, I instantly declined. I remember telling her something along the lines of "I don't like anything here," to avoid seeming like a wimp. After we left Forever 21 without an alarm going off and without anyone saying a word to us, I felt a huge weight lift from my shoulders. But then we stopped at a sunglasses booth and she stole again. Not once did the salesperson glance in our direction. And again we walked away, seemingly unnoticed.

As we headed toward the food court, I heard someone behind us yell, "You stole from my booth." It was the salesperson from the sunglasses booth. Although I was afraid for my friend, I knew I had nothing to hide. Little did I know, it was assumed that *I* was the person who stole the glasses. As the salesperson approached us, my friend who had just told me to "be chill" was now more calm than me because the salesperson had approached me specifically about the stolen item. I knew it was because I was Black. I had seen scenes like this in movies but never imagined those fictional experiences to one day creep up in my own life.

Security was called, and after a few minutes, a white mall security guard came and searched me for the stolen sunglasses. I stood there in the middle of the mall with my arms raised while my friend silently watched, the salesperson insisted the guard "keep checking," and the guard patted my pockets and dug through my bag. At one point, the guard told me I could be arrested if he found the glasses. The embarrassment was more unbearable than the fear of being arrested for something I didn't do. I watched as white patrons walked past the scene, shaking their heads in disapproval at me. My innocence was torn apart at the expense of my friend's privilege.

It turned out that I didn't have any stolen items and that my friend did. But the guard's reaction to finding stolen sunglasses on my friend wasn't the same as assuming stolen sunglasses would be found on me. She wasn't threatened with arrest, she wasn't yelled at, she wasn't made to feel like a criminal. Neither the salesperson nor the guard apologized to me. My friend was let go with a simple verbal warning and we were escorted out of the mall. Not even my friend said sorry for putting me in a dangerous situation. Stupidly, I remained friends with her, and neither of us mentioned the situation to our parents, out of fear that we would have to be supervised the next time we went to the mall. Also out of fear of rejection, I never confronted my friend about the harm she put me in by not taking responsibility for her actions.

Thinking back to the situation at the mall, even if outwardly focused biases led to not one but two adults in the situation believing I had stolen the items, surely the drastic reaction and being told I would be arrested were not only avoidable but inappropriate. It was dehumanizing to see my white friend, who also was a suspect, avoid mistreatment simply because she was the right color in their eyes. I was a child accused of shoplifting no more than thirty dollars' worth of merchandise, yet I was treated like an adult accused of stealing a pricey engagement ring. The situation also made me reflect on my presence. Had my friend gone to the mall with her white girlfriends instead, maybe she wouldn't have encountered a skeptical store clerk or a security guard. In fact, she mentioned to me afterward that she had never been caught stealing before and wondered what went wrong this time. I assumed my Blackness was what went wrong, and so, as a result, she was at risk of being criminalized as well. Although we never talked about it again, I think we both understood the ways in which Black people are vilified simply for existing in our skin.

Throughout my adulthood, occasions where I've been reminded that my experience as a Black woman completely differs from that of my white peers haven't slowed down. Something as simple as booking travel becomes more compli-

cated when my race is factored in. For example, on a few occasions, Airbnb hosts have been extremely questioning when
I've tried to book a stay myself, yet my white friend was not
met with questions when booking the same reservation for us
instead. I've also noticed a stark difference in how willing
people are to help me, acknowledge me, when traveling
abroad with white friends. Even deciding on where to travel
is a task that takes time and research because there are a
plethora of cities that are known to be racist toward Black
people, especially Black women. During a recent optometrist
appointment, the pain I was feeling during the eye examination was consistently dismissed by the doctor. Luckily my
boyfriend, who is white, was in the waiting room, so I texted
him to join me. Once he did, the doctor completely changed
his manner and examined my eye more gently. After the appointment, my boyfriend told me that he had never experienced anything like that in a medical setting, because no one
would have the audacity to dismiss a white man's pain threshold like that. In fact, he said whenever he has expressed concern about something or made medical workers aware that he's
in pain, they've responded with even more care and support
than before. It was, like many other situations in my life, a
reminder that Black women are vilified simply for existing.

When reflecting on the experiences of my childhood and my
encounters with teachers, authoritative figures, and coaches,

I can't help but think of several instances when I was spoken to and treated like I was older than my age, like an adult. Now that I'm older, I'm aware there is a term for that—*adultification bias*. Adultification bias is a form of racial prejudice where children of color, more often Black children, are treated as being more mature than they actually are by a reasonable social standard of development. Adultification of Black girls has placed many young Black girls in dangerous situations during their childhood that typically do not occur even for mature white women during adulthood, exactly like my experience in middle school when I broke up a fight between two girls but was somehow accused of fighting.

When I was in the sixth grade, I made the stupid mistake of trying to break up a fight between my friend Christina and another girl, Kayla. We were in the bathroom in between classes and a heated argument quickly escalated into a verbal combat. Word got around that Kayla had been calling Christina a hoe, so she confronted her about it in the bathroom. I tried to deescalate the situation and hold my friend back as other girls stood around to watch. I don't remember who pushed who first, but when my teacher, Ms. Reitman, rushed into the bathroom, she immediately demanded that Kayla and I go to the office. I yelled, "I wasn't fighting, I was breaking it up." But it didn't matter. Ms. Reitman was not interested in my story. For a moment, I pleaded with her to believe me. Crying, I kept trying to explain that I wasn't the one fighting. Then she yelled at me, told me to shut up and act my age. Never having been sent to the office before, I was terrified of what the consequence would be. At the time, I figured Ms. Reitman didn't send Christina to the office because maybe she truly thought the fight was between Kayla and me. Maybe that's how it looked during the moment she walked in on us. Or maybe another student had told her it was me. While I'm now aware that race played into why I was perceived as combative, at the time I never wondered if Christina being white and Kayla and I both being Black had anything to do with why it was assumed we were the two fighting. I'm lucky that I had a family member who worked for the school district and got me out of the situation after I told him what had happened. I'm even luckier that the incident happened when I was a young kid, in a middle school bathroom, and not an older teen in a public space. Instead of my teacher meeting me with disbelief and sending me to the office, it could have easily been a police officer meeting me with disregard and exerting force, as we have seen time and time again happen to young Black girls who are handled like adults and brutalized by law enforcement. For example, Taylor Bracey was just sixteen years old when she made headlines after being bodyslammed by a school resource officer who was attempting to break up a fight between Bracey and another student. As a result of the excessive force, Bracey was knocked unconscious and suffered a concussion. Not only did the incident leave her traumatized, Bracey has since suffered from memory loss, headaches, blurry vision, and sleep deprivation. This goes to show that adultification of Black girls isn't just a slight from teachers and administration, or even restrained to the school system; it's a bias that can cause permanent psychological damage and effectively change the way Black girls exist in their bodies.

At the time, I couldn't stop thinking of how my teacher shut me down when I advocated for myself and told me to act my age. I had witnessed this same teacher comfort other students who cried over silly things like breaking up with their boyfriend or getting a bad grade on an assignment. But when I cried about being punished for something I didn't do, I wasn't consoled or listened to. I was told to grow up. I was only twelve, yet I was adultified. And this continues to be an issue disrupting the lives of several Black girls to this day.

In January of 2021, I saw a video of a Rochester police officer arresting a nine-year-old Black girl. The cop was responding to a report of "family trouble," and the encounter, which was caught on police body camera videos, showed the little girl crying, to which the police responded, "You're acting like a child." In that moment, it really hit me that the idea that young Black girls are adultified isn't just a stat living in some online study. It happened to me when I was in middle school and is happening to other little Black girls every single day. In the video, the little girl responded, "I am a child!" to the officer, and then was pepper sprayed. With not a moment to spare, without an ounce of humanity afforded to the little girl, the officer predetermined she was not worthy of sanctuary but instead deserved to be treated like an animal.

A 2019 Georgetown Law study titled "Listening to Black Women and Girls: Lived Experiences of Adultification Bias" found that adults were more likely to see white girls as more innocent and vulnerable, eliciting a more protective response. Black girls, on the other hand, are expected to handle conflict in a professional manner, which by white social standards does not involve crying, a change in tone of voice, or signs of frustration. Meanwhile, white girls are often infantilized, even when they're adults.

When season twenty-five *Bachelor* contestant Rachael Kirkconnell was accused of racist behavior in high school and college, attending an antebellum plantation-themed fraternity formal, and liking photos of Confederate flags online, months before pursuing Matt James, the first Black Bachelor, host Chris Harrison pleaded with viewers to forgive her actions and defended her past choices, stating, "People are just tearing this girl's life apart." The twenty-four-year-old *Bachelor* contestant, however, is not a girl; she is an adult, a grown woman, who, like many other white women, was afforded the label "girl" to trivialize her racist past. Her feelings were validated and many fans of the show, along with the show's staff, advocated for her support.

When Black girls are stripped of their innocence during childhood, and perceived and treated like adults, they instantly become victims of dehumanization. A 2017 study conducted by the Georgetown Law Center on Poverty and Inequality found that Black girls as young as five years old are viewed as needing less protection and nurturing than white girls. This unconscious bias not only places targets on Black girls' backs but also subjects them to harsh treatment by police, disbelief from authority, and severe disciplinary action at school.

Adultification is not only about their behavior. Adultification can lead to the hypersexualization of Black girls' bodies as well. When Black girls are treated like adults, and perceived as adults, our bodies, too, are regarded as adult. And when Black girls are hypersexualized, the harm done to them somehow becomes their own fault. Let's take R. Kelly's interactions with Black girls, for instance. R. Kelly has been accused of physically abusing and sexually coercing underage girls since the '90s. When he was later charged for sexually assaulting underage girls in February 2019, the news came as no surprise given his 2008 trial on child pornography charges. While the 2008 verdict found the R & B singer guilty of charges including sexual exploitation of a child, bribery, racketeering, and sex trafficking, one factor that likely contributed to his ability to bypass prosecution despite more than twenty years of alleged abuse of women and underage girls was the fact that the victims are Black. In September 2021, the former singer was found guilty of racketeering and sex trafficking. The conviction came after twenty-five long years of accusations, which received mainstream attention when a 2019 six-hour documentary gave rise to the #MuteRKelly social media movement and caused prosecutors to urge potential witnesses to come forward.

In 2008, a male friend and I were watching an episode of a popular adult cartoon, *The Boondocks*, that focused on R. Kelly, aptly titled "The Trial of Robert Kelly." In the episode, there was a scene of a video of R. Kelly urinating on an under-age girl (which was based on a real video used in the real court case) that the defense showed in court. This scene sparked a jarring conversation between my friend and me. I told him I was disgusted by the singer and surprised that a clip like this made it into a fictional television show. This is when he revealed to me that he held a "middle of the road" stance on the accusations because the girl in the video didn't look fourteen to him. When I asked him how fourteen-year-old girls were supposed to look, he told me, "Not like that," suggesting that because her breasts, thighs, and butt were in development, she had an adult woman body. Despite eleven being the average age for girls to begin puberty, and despite the fact that having a developed body does not have any magical effect on increasing a girl's actual age, my friend was able to unconsciously cast blame on an underage sexual assault victim because of her appearance.

Now, at twenty-seven, I've come to realize how recurring this harmful ideology has been for me and for the Black women I grew up with. I didn't have sex for the first time until I was in college, and most of my friends who held on to their virginity the longest were Black girls. But our sexual innocence was never met with belief when our male class-mates asked us if we were virgins. In fact, no one really ever asked us if we were virgins. It was always presented as some factual statement, like, "I know you definitely be fucking." I didn't understand why it was already predetermined that I was sexually active when there was nothing I said or did to give off that perception. Perhaps because we had larger butts and our skin tone resembled that of the video vixens in music videos where women danced erotically. But my sexual awakening was the complete opposite of what my males peers had assumed. I hadn't even kissed a guy for the first time until the eighth grade, after my friend and I dared each other to. The girls who seemed to have mastered the art of making out, losing their virginity first, and having sex with older guys were always my white girlfriends—and it checks out, not necessarily because they were more promiscuous, but because that's who everyone was most interested in being with.

One friend, Melanie, would invite me to sleep over as a way to distract her parents from the fact that she would sneak guys into her room. I'd sit in her living room at night with the TV on loud, as she would have sex with some senior guy. One morning, after Melanie had snuck in an older guy from a neighboring high school the night before, her mother pulled up a photo on Facebook of another Black girl who went to our school. She was dressed in shorts, smiling, and posing with a guy we knew. Melanie was once best friends with the girl, but the two had gotten into a big argument and stopped talking. I'm sure Melanie's mom was aware of this when she proceeded to tell us, "That girl is so fast and always hanging out with guys. What kind of mother lets their daughter dress like that?" It felt weird hearing a grown woman make unfair assumptions about a young Black girl (who actually had not lost her virginity yet), but it felt even more disturbing knowing that Melanie was one of the most sexually active girls in our class.

Maybe because it was her own daughter, Melanie's mom didn't assume Melanie was fast. But it also spoke volumes that her automatic assumption was that another girl, a Black girl, who dressed very similarly to Melanie, was fast.

Fast and *grown* are both words that are used to label young Black girls as behaving too adultlike or presenting themselves inappropriately, thus blaming them for the harms they endure. These terms place responsibility on young Black girls for the ways their bodies develop and for the inappropriate ways that grown men respond to their bodies. It's a dangerous concept rooted in the premature sexualization of Black girls by adults, and in this case, by my friend's white mother.

In Georgetown Law's 2017 study called "Gender and Trauma," Black girls were found to be viewed by adults as more sexually mature than white girls in the same peer group. When decades of lyrical content suggested that R. Kelly felt age was nothing but a number—when he illegally married fifteen-year-old Aaliyah; when Tiffany Hawkins, a young aspiring singer at the time, sued the artist for "personal injuries and emotional distress" during a three-year relationship that started when she was fifteen and he was twenty-four; when a video of him urinating on an underage girl surfaced across the internet—no one viewed his heinous acts as ones in need of prosecution because the victims were often presented as being responsible for their own assault by asking for it or being groupies. Even in court, victim blaming was a common tactic used against Kelly's victims, despite the fact that many of them were too young to consent. The disbelief that society has toward Black girls who are victims of sexual assault stems from people viewing Black girls as older than they actually are.

When I was younger and still forming most of my opinions, I felt I could control how adults perceived my body. My parents would make me wear shorts from the boys' department because girls' shorts never were long enough to go beyond my knees. I often had to wear one-piece swimsuits because two-piece swimsuits were considered "too mature." These rules seemed heinous at the time, but it was my parents' way of protecting me from being sexualized. And with the modest attire forced upon me, I even viewed other Black girls who would wear short shorts and crop tops that revealed their stomachs as "fast" and "grown." I developed the language from my family members who took pride in covering up their girls and thought clothing choices played a fair role in men's inappropriate and abusive actions toward women. Thankfully, I escaped some level of vitriol from parents and other authority figures because I was thin. Thinness granted me innocence, especially in a Western world that associates curves on Black bodies with hypersexuality. But as we all know, developing large breasts or a plump butt during puberty is completely out of a human's control, and not having either of those does not mean men cannot find you sexually attractive. I think that's what Black girls and women want people to realize—men do not need a reason to hypersexualize anyone. It's out of our control.

Upon realizing that the white girls in my middle school

who wore dresses and short shorts were not perceived as "fast" because of the lack of curves they had or simply because they were white, a color that has always been tied to purity, it was evident that Blackness was more complex than just one experience. All Black women, no matter whether they have light or dark skin, are more susceptible to hypersexualization than non-Black women. But darker-skinned Black women, whose skin tone is furthest away from white on the Pantone scale, and therefore further away from what is considered the equivalent of purity, are more susceptible to hypersexualization than lighter-toned Black women.

During slavery in the United States, before there were as many lighter-skinned Black women as there were darker-skinned counterparts, enslaved African women mostly had dark skin. It was through rape by white slave masters of their African slaves that mixed people with lighter skin became part of the plantation demographic. And while biracial women were also often hypersexualized and subjected to rape and beatings, their white lineage sometimes allowed them to enter relationships with white men, leaving enslavement and plantation life behind. Meanwhile, enslaved, dark-skinned Black women, who did not have white kin, existed to cook, clean, work, reproduce, and fulfill the sexual desires of white men, developing the myth that Black women were seductresses. Today that myth still holds power when young Black girls are called "fast" and "grown" for simply existing, and even more, when curvy and fat Black women, who do not fit the European beauty standard of thinness, are more susceptible to hypersexualization than skinny Black women. While thin Black women, too, are fetishized by non-Black men for being an exception through their straight body type, which is often associated with whiteness, curvy and fat Black women are perceived as sexual objects because of their larger assets, which are often closely aligned to promiscuity in a patriarchal society. Falling within European beauty standards often results in respect and protection by a society that values those standards and equates a woman's beauty to a woman's worth. Whether it be size, skin tone, or hair texture, Black women who do not physically align with Western beauty standards are automatically more susceptible to harm because they are not viewed as worthy of protection. All of this is to say being a young Black woman is to constantly live in a complex world of parallels, where we are degraded and overlooked for our features, yet hypersexualized because of those same features.

I first realized that my body type was perceived differently, more positively, than those of some Black women my age, because of my thinness, when my best friend, Steven, and my roommate at the time, Renee, and I were watching the music video for "Twerk" in our living room. I had joined them on the couch, while FaceTiming with my boyfriend at the time. Both Steven and my roommate were dancing along in their seats to Cardi B and City Girls twerking and rapping on a yacht. I flipped my camera to face the television screen and showed my boyfriend how great the music video was.

"This is so liberating," I exclaimed, which my boyfriend met with, "No, this is ghetto and gross."

Instantly, the vibe in the room changed. My friends overheard his comments and paused the music video. Then they listened quietly as I asked him what he meant by the comment. He said something along the lines of "Twerking is ghetto. I wouldn't feel comfortable knowing my girlfriend is out partying somewhere and doing this. It looks like a mating call." *LOL (what?).* My friends sat there in shock. For a moment, no one knew what to say. He went on to describe it as "practically having sex with your clothes on," to which my roommate responded, "It's just dancing. I doubt your issue is actually with a form of dance and probably has more to do with your disgust for Black women."

Now, I know what you're thinking: How was I dating someone like this? That long-winded answer is for another book but in this moment it is beside the point. The point was that I, too, knew almost instantly that he had this perception because the women doing the dances were Black women. They were curvy women. They were dressed in hip-hop clothing and spewing powerful lyrics. All those components, when put together, were a problem for him, whether he was conscious of it or not.

At the same time, my boyfriend—now my ex—is a white European, and when we would visit his extremely homogeneous hometown, he'd beg me to twerk when we'd go out dancing. He thought it was cool. He saw it as a reason to gloat because—and I mean this in the nicest way possible—none of the girls at these parties knew how to twerk or had a sense of rhythm. It was his form of saying, "Look at my Black American girlfriend who can dance better than anyone here." But it's also equally important that I paint a clear picture of how I look when making the connection between my ex's acceptance of my twerking but disapproval of Cardi B's and the City Girls'. I'm a fairly slim cis woman with a plump butt and nearly nonexistent boobs and am considered tall for a woman and conventionally beautiful by European standards. I do not mention this to gloat or place myself above other women, but more to explain the niche privilege that *I* specifically have as a Black woman. And because of that privilege, my boyfriend saw nothing hypersexual or ghetto about me twerking, the same way he saw nothing hypersexual or ghetto about the models at the Victoria's Secret Fashion Show who posted videos on Instagram of themselves twerking backstage. We share slim, long, cis bodies. For centuries skinny women have been associated with innocence and deserving of admiration, while curvy women, especially curvy Black women, have been perceived as overly sexual beings and nymphomaniacs.

Of course, this realization wasn't news to me. I've been aware of how the Black woman body is perceived through a white gaze for a while now, but it was more chilling to register that even otherwise progressive people often have gaps in their understanding and empathy when it comes to the topic of Black women. My ex would never make these comments about white women, but he was quick to dismiss Black women because of their body type and expression, and even quicker to automatically deem things done by Black women as inherently negative. He found no issue with Lexy Panterra, a notable dancer whom Netflix followed in its *Instafamous* series, for hosting twerking lessons and building a twerk boot camp business. Shortly after videos of her twerking surfaced on the internet, Panterra, a white woman, went viral, was offered business opportunities, and turned her twerking videos into a profitable business of classes and camps. When I showed my ex the episode covering her story and asked him if this was any different than the music video we had just argued about, he couldn't form a valid explanation but in the end concluded, "She turned it into something positive, so it's not the same." And he's right, it isn't the same. Black women, who are the pioneers of twerking, are not usually offered business opportunities or social media stardom when they post videos of themselves dancing online. Instead they're met with backlash and critique, even within their own community. They're hypersexualized, they're called derogatory slurs like "ghetto" and "ratchet," and they aren't afforded respect or support for doing a simple dance that many other women dream of emulating. It's more than annoying to know that you can create something beautiful and the world will view it negatively if you do it, but positively if someone else does, without even acknowledging the hypocrisy of it all.

This all leads me to Megan Thee Stallion and Cardi B's

"WAP" music video. Seemingly anyone who was not a millennial Black woman took issue with the twerking in the video and the sexual nature of the song's lyrics. Critics from all corners condemned the track for its explicit and sexual expression, lamenting the negative influence it would have on young Black girls' sex lives and that it could set Black girls and women back regarding the receiving of love and respect. I mention the general public's response because when Jennifer Lopez and Shakira performed half-naked during the Super Bowl, the world did not critique the negative influence their art form would have on young Latinas; the critique, to the extent there was any, was reserved for the artists themselves and for the entity that gave them a platform. When Miley Cyrus dabbled in hip-hop for one year and started to twerk on her concert stage in revealing two-piece bodysuits, no one worried about the negative influence her expression would have on young white girls specifically; instead they just criticized her and the Disney Channel for the "radical phase" the former *Hannah Montana* star was going through.

When my friend Lauren, a young, white, left-leaning woman, informed me that she understood why people had a problem with the "WAP" music video and that the best way for Black women to avoid this scrutiny is to not give white people a reason to critique them, it was more than apparent that even some highly aware white women, who have studied Black literature, dated non-white men, and are a part of multiracial friend groups, still have much to unlearn in regard to how the Black woman body is perceived. Even one of my somewhat conservative, politically moderate Black friends, Maeve, shared the same sentiments as Lauren. She felt artists like Cardi B and Megan Thee Stallion set Black women back and shouldn't be praised for their expression. In our conversation about the music video, Maeve expressed that when Black women give non-Black people and Black men a reason to hypersexualize us, it furthers the stereotype that we are hypersexual beings and consequently makes it harder for Black women who do not express themselves through vibrant dance or revealing clothing to convince people they are not hypersexual. But what both friends failed to realize is that no matter how a Black woman's body is showcased, our bodies simply aren't perceived the same way other women's bodies are.

I assume Lauren developed her solution to Black women's hypersexualization out of ignorance. After all, she is white and hasn't had the same experience of being part of a demographic that has been historically hypersexualized, for centuries, outside of their control. Maeve's opinions, as a Black woman herself, likely stemmed from respectability politics. As a Black millennial woman, there is often the expectation from older Black women and men that young Black women need to acquiesce to white people and adhere to dominant cultural norms to receive respect. My parents always encouraged me to be on my best behavior, especially when we were in predominantly white spaces, and for good reason. They knew if I made a mistake, it would not be perceived the same way as a mistake my white peers might make, and that it would reflect negatively on their own parenting. But a greater part of respectability politics puts the blame on young Black girls and women and sends a message that there is something wrong with how we naturally look and culturally express ourselves. When adults in our family and community attempt to enforce traditional white norms of femininity on Black girls, it might look like telling us to be softer, quieter, and more ladylike. Other times we're told to alter our look, and that certain hairstyles aren't professional and certain clothing choices are inappropriate. Ultimately, we're being told to be less visible, to be more passive, and to take up less space. We're being told that our Black bodies should only be presented according to white societal standards, lest we be hypersexualized, adultified, degraded, or policed in one way or another.

This is why the public's response to "WAP" is so critical in understanding unconscious biases and the harm and danger done to young Black women. Critiquing "WAP" as degrading, dehumanizing art is a camouflage for critiquing Black womanhood as a problematic expression, especially when there is already so much stacked against us. Black women deserve to reclaim their bodies and advocate for reproductive rights, the freedom of choice, and free expression. Black women deserve to freely use their bodies and express their sexuality how they choose, without extreme judgment, whether through dance, music, clothing, or anything else. While some might find the explicit nature of the "WAP" video to be off-putting and harmful to Black womanhood, the gag itself is that Black women have little to no control over how society views us, with or without Cardi and Megan's collab.

Adultification, hypersexualization, degradation, and policing of our bodies begins as early as our preteen years, and these stereotypes placed on us, which date as far back as colonization, are unavoidable. But Black women shaking their butts and describing their sex lives in music is not what sets Black women back; the problem is the people who would justify harm toward us because of these actions. The problem is the people in positions of authority who don't protect their Black students from harm and harsher treatment because of their skin. The problem is some of the non-Black women who refuse to treat Black women equally or stand up for them because it does not benefit them socially or monetarily. The problem is the lack of care and concern given to Black women and children who encounter sexual assault, criminalization, and invasive policing (by cops or otherwise) because of the ways their bodies are perceived.

Ultimately, Black women just want to receive the same respect, protection, and opportunities as their non-Black counterparts. Black women want non-Black women, and more specifically white women, to be more conscious of the negative ways Black women are perceived and how those biases play out in our livelihood. With this consciousness, they must also actively do anti-racist work within their social circles and families, whether it be educating others about biases or calling out their peers when they are perpetuating stereotypes that harm Black women. But most importantly, they must self-reflect and acknowledge their own blind spots, while simultaneously counteracting them by making space for, showing up for, and passing along opportunities to Black women. Until this version of "doing the work" becomes a constant practice in our society, the conditions that follow being a young woman in a Black body will remain unequal and regressive.

CHAPTER 2

Leave the Box Braids for the Black Girls

The summer before I went into the third grade, my mom allowed me to get my first relaxer. No longer would I be teased by the kids in my class for having kinky hair. I thought having a relaxer would magically turn my hair into white-girl hair, and since no one made white girls feel like their hair was ugly or untamed, I would be saved from any more bullying. Once I had joined the relaxed-hair group, only one Black girl (of the five Black girls in my class), Jackie, had natural hair. While Jackie experienced being told her hair was ugly and nappy, the other Black girls and I acclimated easily and made friends with non-Black girls quickly. Even when Jackie wore her hair in braids, some of the kids in our class would tell her she looked like a boy, or that braids were ugly. So, when my mom would offer to get my hair braided in the summers, I would avoid it at all costs. Through the bullying I witnessed natural-haired Black girls experience, I was learning to hate my own

God-given hair. So of course it was confusing for me to visit the homes of my white friends and see photos of them with their hair in cornrows from their family trips to Mexico or Jamaica. This acceptance of braids on themselves, as a fun hairdo to sport on vacation, but repudiation of the hairdo as a protective style on Black girls was my earliest encounter with cultural appropriation.

I had no idea that this phenomenon of non-Black people borrowing my culture would become a norm throughout my adulthood, exacerbated by others' access to Black womanhood, style, and expression through the media. I also didn't realize how Black features and expression could be monopolized, create opportunities and desirability for others, and quite literally push non-Black people who engage in Black culture to the top of the social ladder. As an "online" Black woman, I witness this often. Whether it be our facial expressions and mannerisms, the slang and phrases we use, our hair and clothing styles, or our cultural practices and norms, the internet has allowed others access to us without crediting us, befriending us, holding relationships with us, and sharing opportunities with us. It blurs the lines of what is appropriate and what is not, what is professional and what is not. What is cultural or natural to me is often deemed unprofessional, unattractive, and inappropriate by non-Black people, but then trendy or interesting when non-Black people present it themselves. The hypocrisy in how the world takes from and capitalizes off Black womanhood but gives Black women nothing in return, and then fights with us when we express our anger about this, is frustrating, to say the least.

One such infuriating time, after my first encounter with cultural appropriation, was in middle school, when I was ridiculed for having full lips. Two specific white girls in my class would joke about how large they were, pushing me to hate what has become one of my most attractive physical attributes as I've gotten older. Later, in high school, one white girl, Virginia, announced in front of everyone that I should get lip reduction surgery. In her opinion, my lips were too large. At the time, her opinion mattered to me because she was the popular girl whom all the guys liked. Simultaneously, Virginia had photos of Angelina Jolie and Adriana Lima in her locker. I couldn't understand why full lips on me were unattractive to her, but not on the faces of her white idols. The bullying went so far that I eventually googled the cost of lip-reduction surgery. It was affordable, but I was immediately terrified by the thought of a surgeon removing fat from my lips with a scalpel and scissors. I'm lucky that the surgery videos disgusted me, because I can't for sure say I wouldn't have gone through with it had I been older and had the resources at the time. Similar to how some teens might take on harmful diets or develop eating disorders from being bullied about their weight, or how some women of darker skin tones have used bleaching creams to lighten their complexion because fair skin is considered more desirable in their culture, I wanted to get rid of the full lips that were causing me so much insecurity. But today it's almost impossible to scroll through my Instagram feed and not pass through numerous images of non-Black women with artificial, heavily lined, fuller lips than mine. It's almost impossible to not feel some fury when remembering how these same kinds of women made me feel less than about my natural beauty.

Speaking of natural beauty and cultural appropriation, I should mention my favorite movie growing up was *Bring It On*. I thought Gabrielle Union was the most beautiful woman I had ever seen, and her character seemed relatable to my friends and me. In the film, the East Compton Clovers, led by Union, show up to a football game and witness San Diego's Rancho Carne Toros performing their cheer routine, step by step. Outraged, the Clovers then begin to perform their stolen routine simultaneously with the Toros, so loudly and so exceptionally that the Toros, out of embarrassment, stop performing the routine altogether. The classic scene is popular for its you-got-served undertones but acts as an example of white people capitalizing on Black culture.

While the Clovers took home gold in the national cheer-leading competition, it's only in a fictional movie that Black women, the original creators of the routine, who effortlessly and exceptionally perform it, were credited for their contributions. In real life, it plays out quite differently.

When Jalaiah Harmon's Renegade dance blew up on Tik-Tok, it wasn't until *The New York Times* reported her as the creator, in February 2020, that she started to gain momentary, widespread recognition. Prior to the news article, Tik-Tok star Charli D'Amelio was deemed the dance's captain for popularizing it, was offered business opportunities and TV guest appearances, and gained social media fame for a less-expressive version of Harmon's routine. Celebrities like Lizzo, David Dobrik, and Kourtney Kardashian all performed the dance on their respective TikTok accounts, speaking to the viral nature of the challenge. Nearly a year later, TikTok star Addison Rae performed eight viral dance challenges on *The Tonight Show* without crediting any of their original choreographers, many of whom happen to be Black. But the Fallon show performance wasn't the first time a white TikToker received preferential treatment and business opportunities for dances they didn't create. During NBA All-Star Weekend 2020, the NBA invited several white TikTok creators, including Rae and siblings Charli and Dixie D'Amelio, to be interviewed, watch the game from prime seats, and teach NBA cheerleaders and players TikTok dances on the court, one of those dances being the Renegade.

Similar to the way the Toros stole the Clovers' cheer in *Bring It On*, several "online" non-Black girls and women have been imitating Black style and expression for years, reaping the benefits while rarely paying homage to, or sharing their opportunities with, the women who influenced them. The parallels between the fictional teen comedy and real life are too close to deny. In *Bring It On*, the Toros cheerleading team had a history of spying on the Clovers' rehearsals. In the East Compton High School scene, Missy and Torrance show up to the gym at East Compton High School and are shocked to find that a predominantly Black team is rehearsing the cheers the Toros spent years learning. What relates even more is the conversation between Gabrielle Union's character, Isis, and Torrance, played by Kirsten Dunst. "Y'all been coming up for years trying to jack us for our routines," Isis says. Then her co-cheerleader states, "And we just love seeing them on ESPN." When an ignorant Torrance seems confused by their sentiments, Isis goes further, arguing that there's no way Torrance actually thought a white girl wrote "Brr, It's Cold in Here"—which is completely valid, given that the cheer steps and chants are heavily related to steps and chants used by Black fraternities and sororities. She continues, "It's like every time we get some, here y'all come trying to steal it, put some blond hair on it and call it something different."

In 2000, pop culture still hadn't begun to grapple with the phenomenon of cultural appropriation in the mainstream. *Bring It On* was ahead of its time. The Toros stole the cheers from the Clovers, knowing they were better than what they could create on their own, and won competitions by using them. Dishearteningly, the Toros not only were unaware that the captains before them were stealing the routines, but always appeared to be in a state of utter disbelief. For them, ignorance was synonymous with absolution, but as Gabrielle

Union told ESPN in an interview about the film, "You are still benefiting from the labor of someone else. Your white privilege is buoyed by that. Whether you are conscious of that or not, the reality is that you have gained privileges from your whiteness. You don't get to claim ignorance."

It's also crucial to acknowledge the intersectionality of cultural appropriation, which is explored so thought-provokingly by Anna P. Kambhampaty in her *New York Times* article about Raven Sutton, a Black dancer and American Sign Language (ASL) performer who aims to make "mainstream music accessible to the Deaf/HOH [hard of hearing] community." In 2021, Sutton translated "WAP" into an ASL dance, taking special care to choose signs and movements that really captured the tone and spirit of the song as much as the nuance of the literal words. Sutton's video was posted to her social media channels, but it was a white hearing interpreter, Kelly Kurdi, who went viral for an ASL "WAP" interpretation performed at Lollapalooza—her dance getting more than fourteen million views on TikTok. While Kurdi did and does credit Black ASL creators in her social media posts and has publicly acknowledged the impact Sutton's "WAP" dance had on her own, Sutton points out the potential harmful loss inherent in a white person's interpretation of a song by a Black creator: "They are signing songs that are not of their culture.... This is a hip-hop song talking about a Black experience of a Black thing, but we got a white face who's gone viral, so white people are getting the glow up off these types of things." While Sutton and Kurdi have both had such positive impacts on the visibility of Deaf/HOH people in the arts, it's disheartening to see yet another example of Black content being overshadowed by a white imitation or interpretation.

With social media acting as a digital aid in providing access to Black culture—whether it be TikTok dances, the word *chile* or other African American Vernacular English (AAVE) colloquialisms, or traditionally Black hairstyles like box braids—millennial and Gen Z Black women are witnessing their identity being imitated and stolen, while simultaneously watching the women appropriating their culture reap fame and exposure for their copying. A TikTok dance might seem like a minor example, given that the platform is fair use and anyone posting to it risks their creation being used by other people. But the issue isn't so much with someone seeing a dance, being inspired by it, and then replicating it on their own account. The issue is with the opportunities afforded to these people, because the dance is now being presented by a white body. Until brands and companies are willing to step up and provide opportunities for Black creators, then the onus does fall on non-Black creators to start a conversation about who is being left out. Both D'Amelio and Rae rose to fame by copying dances from Black creators, the same Black creators who rarely reach their level of success. Not only have these two white TikTok stars become millionaires in less than two years of being on the platform, but the original versions of the dances they copied are always inarguably performed better by the creators and other Black TikTok users. So what exactly pushes them to the top? If it isn't their exceptional dance moves, or their own creativity, then perhaps it's their physique. Both women are young, conventionally beautiful by Western standards, and, most importantly, white. They don't have to be able to twist and move like the original creators, they don't even have to create the dances themselves, they just have to fit the look that society has deemed beautiful, profitable, and valuable. It's hard to imagine what these TikTok stars would do if Black creators stopped posting for a year. Where would they get their ideas from? Who would inspire them? Would their careers even be sustainable? Actually, Black creators on TikTok tested it out. In June 2021, Megan Thee Stallion's "Thot Shit" grew in popularity, quickly becoming the song of the summer. It was bound to become a TikTok dance challenge for its catchy chorus and hip-hop beat, but Black TikTok creators had already decided they would not be creating a dance for it. The strike was created to protest the lack of credit given to Black creators for their creativity and original work on the app. Using the hashtag "BlackTikTokStrike" on TikTok, Black creators began sharing unsuccessful videos of non-Black creators attempting to create dance challenges in the absence of Black creators, raising awareness of the strike.

In April of 2021, *Bustle* profiled Addison Rae as a TikTok star worth knowing about, even if you're a millennial. I only recognized her name because a month earlier the drama surrounding her performing stolen dances by Black creators on *The Tonight Show* made me think that surely the media would highlight some of the Black creators who went unnoticed. When asked about the situation, in the last paragraph of the lengthy essay, Rae responded, "It's kind of hard to credit during the show, but they all know that I love them so much and, I mean, I support all of them so much." This was embarrassingly passive since it would have been extremely easy to credit the creators during the show by simply adding their TikTok handle under the dance's name. And regarding support, it's hard to imagine how exactly Rae is supporting a group of people who, at the time of the interview, she had not met up with, though she has been using their dances for clout since joining TikTok. As a former member of the TikTok collective Hype House, you would think Rae would have already invited the creators to collaborate with her in person, as she has with several other white TikTok stars. Or talk about sharing brand opportunities with them. But no. Instead, as she told *Bustle*, "Hopefully one day we can all meet up and dance together." Luckily, someone is looking to credit the creators that Rae hopes to one day meet and dance with. In April 2021, just a month after the backlash, JaQuel Knight, a choreographer famous for Beyoncé's "Single Ladies" and Megan Thee Stallion's virtual concert, launched Knight Choreography and Music Publishing Inc., a company that copyrights dance moves.

As a twenty-six-year-old who found herself becoming highly frustrated with TikTok's white-centering algorithms and penchant for monopolizing Black culture, I refrained from posting on the app altogether for a while. But it's not like I haven't seen non-Black women imitate Black women outside of sixty-second video clips before. I've observed celebrities and non-Black women whom I follow on Instagram gradually transition into ethnic ambiguity over the course of two years by filling their lips, giving their hair braid-outs, tanning their skin, and outlining their pout with lip liner. By slicking their hair back into a tight low bun, cutting unnatural baby hairs and gelling them down, performing winged eyeliner to give them "fox eyes," and accentuating their look with style norms of predominantly Black neighborhoods, like large-hooped earrings and hip-hop clothing, suddenly a generically pretty canvas is turned into an ethnically ambiguous portrait. Actually, this popular look, which often entails slicked-back buns, gold hoops, and dewy, moisturized skin, has recently been coined the "clean girl aesthetic." Despite these beauty "tricks" existing as staples in Black and brown women's fashion for decades, their newfound popularity is highly represented by white women. Bella Hadid and Hailey Bieber are frequently coined the celeb pioneers of the aesthetic, but Black celebrities like Alicia Keys, Solange, Justine Skye, and Megan Thee Stallion have been sporting it for years. In this age, Black traits and culture adapted by white women have proven to lead to success in entertainment careers, desirability by men, and separation from whiteness. In fact, Black expression and culture have always been valuable when adopted by our non-Black counterparts, but that adoption hasn't always been as easy to challenge.

In the early 2000s, before social media platforms allowed

for global discussions, people were far less aware of and willing to call out cultural appropriation than they are now. When Gwen Stefani released her 2004 album *Love. Angel. Music. Baby.*, her song "Harajuku Girls" and the accompanying entourage of Japanese women who were hired to follow her around were defended as a "literal bow down to a culture that I was a superfan of." Prior to her Harajuku days, Stefani frequently sported a bindi, a forehead decoration that is culturally and spiritually significant for South Asian women. Throughout the '90s, the singer often appeared wearing Bantu knots and cornrows. Originating from the Zulu tribes in South Africa and notoriously recognized as a Black protective hairstyle, Bantu knots soon were mainstreamed as "mini buns" and are still often attributed to Stefani as a '90s beauty trend she cultivated. And then there was her chola phase. In her 2005 music video "Luxurious," Stefani appropriates Mexican American culture through her clothing choices and overall appearance. Debuting thinly drawn-on eyebrows and thickly lined lips, the white artist can easily be mistaken for a Mexican American woman. The extras in the video are all Mexican American, and Stefani, the blondest and whitest woman on camera, is leading the show. But imitating women of different backgrounds is only part of the problem. The other and more frustrating half is the denial of something so overwhelmingly obvious. When criticized by the media for her various phases of emulating non-white cultures, Stefani has acted aloof, denied engaging in appropriation, and claims she was heavily influenced by the respective different cultures during different periods in her upbringing. In fact, Stefani's understanding of, or more so, comfort with, engaging in cultural appropriation hasn't seemed to change despite being called out time and time again. In 2022, she was called out for sporting dreadlocks in Sean Paul's "Light My Fire" music video, showing no remorse for the backlash from her earlier days.

Whiteness entirely confers the privilege of being ignorant, and whiteness allows women like Stefani, when confronted with the truth, to skirt the difficulty of reckoning with their complicity. But even prominent women of other races, who are not white, have adopted culturally Black vernacular and expression to boost their careers and refuse to take accountability when called out about it. Take Awkwafina, for example, a very successful Asian actress and comedian who grew her fame by employing a blaccent in her roles and expressing herself through culturally Black jargon and slang. If one were to hear Awkwafina's voice-over without an image or name tied to it, it would be safe to assume she was a Black woman— that's how deeply rich her minstrel act is. It's widely known that African American vernacular, the use of Black slang, and Ebonics are frowned upon, so much so that Black people often have learned to code-switch in order to receive opportunities and fair treatment or advance in their career. But for Awkwafina, a woman who is not Black, the use of AAVE pronounced in a culturally Black drawl is comical, entertaining, and different. It's deserving of a successful career in film because it provides the same entertainment as a Black woman but in a more culturally acceptable body. Meanwhile, when Black women present this way, it produces the opposite effect. Tiffany Haddish is one such actress; she has been criticized for her vocabulary and viewed as ghetto and uneducated—while Awkwafina is considered a talented actress with *street credibility*. And like Stefani, when Awkwafina has been asked about her cultural appropriation, she denies that it is problematic and doesn't issue an apology. In a 2021 interview, instead of acknowledging the success her use of a blaccent has brought her, or its cultural insensitivity, she described it as "multifaceted" and "layered," all while saying this in her natural tone of voice, without the use of the blaccent or AAVE she is so popularly known for. It's also been highlighted that Awkwafina's use of a blaccent has died down since she began obtaining more serious roles that do not rely on a comedic character, furthering the idea that Blackness is comical and showcasing Awkwafina's ability to drop her use of Blackness when it's no longer bringing her success. The blaccent isn't multifaceted, but *she* gets to be multifaceted. The blaccent isn't layered, but her use of it is layered in historically racist minstrelsy. When celebrities like Awkwafina and Stefani, with massive platforms, refuse to acknowledge Black culture as an influence that benefits their careers, it eradicates opportunities for Black women and makes other non-Black women feel like cultural appropriation is okay.

In popular culture and fashion, Black women's style and swag are often stolen by and then praised on their white counterparts, rendering Black women invisible, or worse, denigrated for the very things white people have stolen from them.

Minh-Ha T. Pham, an associate professor in the Graduate Program in Media Studies at Pratt Institute, would declare the practice neither cultural appropriation nor cultural appreciation, but rather racial plagiarism. In her essay "Racial Plagiarism and Fashion," she argues that cultural appreciation gives too much weight to the stealer's feelings and casts anyone who calls them out as a "hater," while cultural appropriation too quickly reduces the problem to one of utility. Meanwhile, plagiarism, by definition, is presenting someone else's work or ideas as your own, with or without their consent, by incorporating it into your work without full acknowledgment. Plagiarism benefits the plagiarizer but never the originator.

We've seen this play out before, specifically during Marc Jacobs's spring/summer 2017 show at New York Fashion Week, when a predominantly white lineup of fashion models sported fake dreadlocks on the runway. The popular Rastafarian hairstyle has been criticized in the media as dirty and dreadful. Employees at some businesses were even previously banned from sporting the hairstyle at work. But that evening, at fashion's largest event, locks were considered fashionable and innovative. When Jacobs's hair stylist Guido Palau was asked if Rasta culture inspired the hairstyle, Palau responded, "No, not at all." Instead, he referenced "the '80s, raver culture, Boy George, and Harajuku." The stylist's omission of dreadlocks in the context of Black culture is an erasure far too common when non-Black people partake in historically and culturally Black expression.

Because of the internet and social media, there's now more

opportunity to partake in cultural appropriation because of extreme access to different cultures. As Pham puts it, "Racial masquerade and racial tourism... are part and parcel of internet history. The internet—dating back to when people were still calling it the 'world wide web' or 'cyberspace'—has always promised computer users, who were tacitly white, the promise of trying on different identities." And in the digital age, it's transcended to digital blackface, a practice that allows non-Black people to more easily claim Black identity without identifying as Black through the use of racially ambiguous face filters, Black GIFs and voice-overs, language, and blaccents. What might seem harmless and funny to some is perpetuating racist stereotypes of Black people being loud, combative, and overly animated. The practice itself is closely aligned with minstrelsy, in which non-Black people pair sound bites featuring Black voices with exaggerated expressions and gestures for comic effect. It's a huge problem among non-Black Gen Z and younger millennial users on TikTok and can negatively impact Black women more than any other demographic. In an article titled "What Is Digital Blackface? Experts Explain Why the Social Media Practice Is Problematic," Keri Kirk, PhD, a clinical psychologist at MedStar Georgetown University Hospital, argues, "When Black women see non-Black people being valued for emulating trends or characteristics made popular by Black women, but they themselves do not obtain that same recognition, it can negatively impact mental health." She goes on to claim that "these issues are rooted in minstrelsy not just in the nature of the performance itself, but also in that white performers are profiting both socially and financially off of the likenesses of Black people. On TikTok, the most popular creators can make thousands of dollars per post, and they often use choreography, audio, and mannerisms made popular by Black personalities to do so."

From Bhad Bhabie to members of the Kardashian/Jenner family, white and non-Black pop stars who take on Black expression and style and claim it as their own to build a more lucrative career are a leading influence in the cultural co-opting we see happening on social media and in the real world. They make excuses about their expression, saying, "I grew up listening to hip-hop, so that's why I dress like this," or "I grew up around Black people so that's why I talk like this," or "This is how dark my skin gets when I tan" (despite utilizing self-tanners), yet as soon as the act is no longer serving them, suddenly they have the tools and knowledge to re-brand back to white. A great example of this is the ever-changing career of Miley Cyrus. In 2013, Cyrus transitioned from a country and pop singer to a twerking hip-hop artist, with hopes to skyrocket her career. When rap failed to work for the *Hannah Montana* star, she refuted the genre altogether, claiming that "it was too much 'Lamborghini, got my Rolex, got a girl on my cock'—I am so not that." After gyrating onstage during performances, twerking in a high school bathroom in the "23" music video, and collabing with male rap artists like Wiz Khalifa and Juicy J while wearing a Chicago Bulls bra and booty shorts, Cyrus discovered that her image was scrutinized as vulgar and hypersexual. People were upset that she participated in hip-hop culture in the first place. The media did not believe it was respectable for a white former Disney star like her to express herself this way. As a result of the backlash, she dropped the act. Cyrus was able to "try on" a culturally Black aesthetic and then reclaim her image by deciding she was done with rap, or Black culture, when it no longer served her.

Since the rise of Instagram, a new form of physical cultural appropriation has grown in popularity among non-Black women who make cosmetic alterations or edit their photos in ways that present themselves as less European-looking, racially ambiguous, or of mixed ancestry. The phenomenon has a name: blackfishing. Coined in 2018 by journalist Wanna Thompson after she realized a new wave of white women was cosplaying as Black women on social media, blackfishing describes someone who is accused of pretending to be Black on social media by using makeup, hair products, and in some cases surgery to drastically alter their appearance to achieve a Black or mixed-race look. With the additions of deep self-tanner and filler-injected lips, coupled with manipulated hairstyles and wigs, and sometimes surgery to widen the hips or enlarge the butt, the previous look of white women with naturally pale skin, classic European facial features, thin bodies, and straight hair has transformed into a look that appears mixed-raced of some sort. Some Instagram influencers, like Swedish model Emma Hallberg, @emmahallberg (who is infamous for being the first documented example of the practice of blackfishing), have been able to fool their fans, white and Black, into believing they are not white. Meanwhile, some non-Black celebrities, like Kylie Jenner and Ariana Grande, have quietly adopted the look, causing some fans to associate their sudden change in features with puberty as opposed to some of the alterations found in blackfishing.

Thompson blames access through the media. In an article for *Paper* magazine, she writes, "White women have been able to steal looks and styles from Black women, more specifically styles that Black women in lower-economic communities have pioneered. With the help of the media, white women have been credited profusely for creating several 'trends' that have existed long before they discovered them. What makes this 'phenomenon' alarming is that these women have the luxury of selecting which aspects they want to emulate without fully dealing with the consequences of Blackness."

Whether someone goes as far as lying about their race, or undergoes cosmetic procedures and adopts certain expressions to pass as non-white, the portrayal capitalizes off the "exotic" looks of historically oppressed minorities. Most women who take part in blackfishing are in denial, and maybe that's because, unlike historical blackface performers, the perpetrators are not performing it with the explicit intention of mocking and ridiculing Black people; nevertheless, it is exploitative and wrong. Not only that, but it actively takes away representation and opportunities from Black women. It also encourages fetishism of another person's appearance, so much that the blackfishing person is willing to go to great lengths to adopt the appearance themselves. In the same way some non-Black men have been known to fetishize Black women, some of their female counterparts are doing the same through their appropriation of their looks and expression. The only difference is that the fetishism is not romantic or sexual, nor nearly as verbally explicit, but it is present in their cosmetic decisions and style choices. Fetishism *is* to have an excessive and irrational commitment to or obsession with something or someone. And when non-Black women are so heavily influenced by Black women's expression, word choices, articulation, clothing sense, hairstyles, and physical attributes—a phenomenon that is rarely a two-way street—obsession is the only explanation. Picking which parts of Black women they want to copy, and not dealing with the negative experiences that come with actually being a Black woman online or in real life, suggests that some women view Blackness as lucrative. Furthermore, their gain is through social media, where these same white women have been credited abundantly for starting trends that were pioneered mostly by young Black women with fewer resources. As Thompson laid out so eloquently for *Paper* magazine, "What makes this both so harmful and insulting is that Black women have to work twice as hard to obtain the same, if not fewer, benefits as white women in these spaces, so when white influencers are rewarded with partnerships and brand sponsorships under the pernicious guise that they are racially ambiguous women, it's beyond infuriating." The same Black aesthetic that some white and non-Black women try to emulate is an aesthetic that many dark-skinned Black women are still shunned for having all on their own, like rarely being represented in the media for having dark skin while watching white women become more desirable from darkening their skin. What these women fail to realize is that they want access to Blackness but don't want the suffering that comes along with it and don't even have the consciousness to acknowledge how Blackness has molded so much of their aesthetic. Frustratingly, so many of these celebrities and everyday women appear silent or do the bare minimum when issues of racial injustice occur, suggesting they strive to emulate only these women's aesthetic, but not their values. Whether or not their participation in blackfishing and cultural appropriation is done with ill intent, they want to receive accolades and privileges for appearing racially ambiguous and holding street knowledge while remaining socially, politically, and constitutionally white.

When Black women bring up these frustrations, with women co-opting our existence and benefiting from it in ways we don't benefit ourselves, we are often perceived as jealous or bitter. To this, I respond, is it surprising at all that a marginalized group is frustrated by seeing white women who already have a social and cultural advantage be rewarded for appropriating features that marginalized groups are routinely ridiculed or passed on for? I don't think any Black women are jealous of women who try to look like Black women, but instead are pissed off by the social, cultural, and financial ease that comes with being a white person partaking in blackfishing, especially on the internet. So long as people appropriate us, we have the right to point it out. As Thompson said, "Black women are constantly bombarded with the promotion of European beauty standards in the media, so when our likeness is then embraced on women who have the privilege to fit traditional standards yet freely co-opt Blackness to their liking, it reaffirms the belief that people desire Blackness, just not on Black women."

Personally, I believe most culture appropriators do feel a genuine appreciation for whatever aspect of a culture they are appropriating and hold a lack of awareness of the harm it causes—yet that doesn't excuse their actions. Cultural appropriation is more loaded than appreciation or borrowing—it creates an imbalanced power relationship between the person of a dominant group (often a white person) and the marginalized group they claim to be inspired by. It also affects how the marginalized group is perceived, and how they perceive themselves. What many people who play into cultural appropriation don't see is the healing journey many young Black women have had to go on to come to the conclusion that there's nothing wrong with how we look or express ourselves; society just glorifies it when displayed on other women. Many of us have had to do inner work with loving, appreciating, and accepting the same features and cultural norms we've been tormented and rejected for in childhood, only to see other women receive praise for embodying our existence. Ultimately, cultural appropriation is not a compliment, but rather a thing that takes opportunities away from Black women and provides them less representation and space to be their authentic selves.

More importantly, cultural appropriation is about entitlement. It's about noticing something that is cool, attractive, or lucrative about someone else and feeling entitled to reap the benefits of it too—in most cases, more benefits than its originator will ever receive. If people, brands, and companies are going to continue to use Black womanhood and Black culture as the blueprint driving their success, then at the very least, involve, pay, and support Black women in the process.

CHAPTER 3

Why Are You So Dark?

I quit tennis during the most important year of my high school career. I was a sophomore at South Grand Prairie High School and had just wrapped up my second term on varsity. Colleges in Florida and Pennsylvania had expressed their interest in me, and I already had two school visits planned. Anyone who has seriously competed in high school sports knows that sophomore year is scouting year and junior year is signing year, and since I was the only freshman girl to join varsity, I knew I was on the right track. But by the end of spring season in 2011, I was ready to give up my favorite sport of all time—if that meant forgoing a tan.

For as long as I can remember, I was critical of and criticized about my dark skin. Sometimes the jokes were made by peers, but more often by close friends and sometimes even family members—people whom I trusted and should have felt safe around. The more I was teased, the more upset I grew with being a dark-skinned Black girl. One summer, right before entering high school, I went swimming with my best friend, my crush, and his friends. After three hours of being outside, my skin, like everyone else's, got a tan. When we all went inside the local recreation club to get dressed, my crush, who was darker than me, made a comment along the lines of "Whoa, Brianna, I didn't know you could actually get any darker." Seeing my best friend, my crush's friends, but most of all, my crush laughing at me for getting darker made me no longer want to swim for the rest of the summer. I remember feeling like there was no way that the guy I liked would ever like me back. In his eyes, I was probably "too dark" for him. From then on, I missed out on summers filled with swimming at the neighborhood pool with my friends unless it was indoors or a cloudy day, just to avoid getting darker.

When you're a child, restricting yourself to being indoors means bypassing a plethora of transformative experiences, but I had convinced myself that missing out on having fun was far better than getting darker and being teased. I didn't think of the sun as dangerous because it could cause cancer or prematurely age skin. I thought of it as my enemy because it had the power to cause others to think I was ugly, unattractive, or less than. Yes, those were actual sentiments coming out of my peers' mouths—and, more importantly, the collective voice of my own community. Those words were fueled by colorism.

Colorism is defined as prejudice or discrimination against

individuals with a dark skin tone, and favoritism toward individuals with lighter skin, typically among people of the same ethnic or racial group. For the Black community, and even other communities of color, combating colorism has been a serious emotional and psychological battle for decades. But it isn't limited to the intraracial situations we often think of when discussing colorism. Colorism is also a systemic issue that runs rampant in education, corporate workspaces, healthcare, and policing, putting people of darker complexion behind and sometimes in dangerous situations. For example, dark-skinned Black students are more likely to experience unfair disciplinary action and are more likely to be prevented from taking more advanced courses in educational settings; dark-skinned Black people hold a lower socioeconomic status and are less likely to hold elected office compared to their lighter-skinned counterparts; dark-skinned Black students are more vulnerable to incarceration than light-skinned Black students; dark-skinned Black women receive sentences that are 12 percent longer than light-skinned Black women; and relative darkness of skin tone could increase the likelihood of being shot and killed by police while unarmed. In fact, sociologists Verna Keith and Cedric Herring, in their research on the effects of colorism, have found that skin tone is a significant predictor of net income, education level, occupation, urbanicity, parental socioeconomic status, and even marital status. Within the labor market, for example, while Black workers with medium and dark complexions earned 26.5 and 34.5 percent less than white workers, respectively, the wage differential between white workers and light-skinned Black workers was so small that studies found it to be a nonfactor. Additionally, within the criminal justice system, studies have proven that the more "stereotypically Black" a defendant appears—someone possessing a darker skin tone and Afro-centric facial features—the more the chances of being sentenced to death increase. The chance of being stopped and/or arrested by police and of receiving longer sentences is higher for dark-skinned Black people as compared to light-skinned Black people. In terms of education levels, the gap between light-skinned and dark-skinned Black people in the same age-group is wider than that of the education-level gap between Black people and white people in the same age-group. Specifically, according to data drawn from the National Health Interview Survey (2005), white Americans between age twenty-five and forty-five have 10.2 months more education on average than Black Americans. By contrast, according to data drawn from the National Survey of American Life (2001–2003), the education gap between lighter-skinned and darker-skinned Black Americans between ages twenty-five and forty-four is 15.4 months. In other words, the significant educational inequality between Black and white people mirrors that within the Black population along the color continuum. All of this data shows that there has not been much improvement in dismantling the systemic issues of colorism from the data collected in the 1980 National Survey of Black Americans to the present day.

Ultimately, colorism creates harmful stereotypes and biases

for dark-skinned members of one racial group, while doing the complete opposite for lighter-skinned members of the same group. Research shows that in the Black community, light-skinned people are more likely to garner empathy, sympathy, and support from others. The behaviors people tolerate from lighter people are often the same behaviors that darker people are punished for. Similar to the ways in which racism disadvantages Black people but advantages white people, colorism disadvantages darker people but advantages lighter people. Also, similar to how some white people will deny racism if it isn't overt, or refute their own role in racism, some Black people and non-Black people deny the existence of colorism and the ways in which they perpetuate the discrimination. What I've found when talking with people who have expressed colorist beliefs is that although they were more overt about their colorist beliefs, in the form of teasing, during their youth than in their adulthood, many of them deny the existence of colorism at all or seem to have forgotten that they used colorist remarks when they were younger. Even the word *colorism* is not recognized grammatically in most English keyboards, suggesting the behavior is not widely acknowledged or believed, yet it is a real discriminatory practice that darker-skinned Black people, specifically darker-skinned Black women, are constantly subjected to.

When I was younger I had very little awareness of the negative impact colorism was having on my self-perception and the body dysmorphia it would instill throughout my adolescence. But by middle school it became obvious to me that the non-Black boys in my class were not physically attracted to me or other dark-skinned girls because of our dark skin, although they never had to verbalize it. By choosing to only flirt with white girls, non-Black girls, and lighter-skinned Black girls, they made it obvious that the shade of my skin did not fit within their range of attractiveness. At the time, I didn't realize it wasn't really their fault they held these preferences or acted on their unconscious ideas of ideal beauty. But now I see that they were influenced by a society filled with colorist media and rhetoric.

My Black peers, however, both boys and girls, were more forward and vocal about their distaste for dark skin. Even the Black girls who were only a shade or two lighter than me took pride in not being the darkest person in the room, speaking to the self-hate that is bred into dark-skinned girls by their own communities from birth. I started to see my skin as something grotesque. Despite how flawless my complexion was and how smooth my skin felt, when I looked in the mirror or down at my arms, I couldn't help but wish I would magically wake up multiple shades lighter.

I distinctly remember my friends and me lining up the outside of our forearms together to decide who was darker. Often my arm would take the win for being the darkest, but the triumph was not one to celebrate. These absurd tests placed our skin tones on a figurative hierarchy throughout middle school and high school but became less blatant over time.

Instead, my attractiveness and value were determined through comparisons to other Black people. If I was darker than someone, then they were prettier, and if I was lighter than someone, then I was saved from being cast as the ugly person. Despite my peers' opinions, I think deep down I believed I must be somewhat beautiful. I was tall, I was constantly scouted by modeling agents during outings, and by my senior year of high school, I had even won a beauty pageant. I was thin, and I fit many other conventional beauty standards, but my dark skin tone had ways of washing those features out for others. And so, because my skin tone was considered ugly to so many of the people around me, I started to believe it too.

Once, when sleeping at my house in high school, my Mexican friend Carolina said, "Bri, you would be so much prettier if you were as light as your mom." At the time, Carolina thought this was a compliment, and the conversation still leaves a weight in my heart. I forced a smile to make her feel comfortable in a situation where she made me uncomfortable, as I did several other times when my skin tone was criticized by my peers. Luckily my mom confronted Carolina's ignorance and told her that I was beautiful regardless, and that disrespectful comments like that would not be allowed in her home. Carolina apologized, but I could tell she didn't understand why her comment was problematic. She didn't really know *what* she was apologizing for. Thinking that I would be prettier if I were lighter *is* how she truly felt. While she was sorry for offending me with the statement and was embarrassed for being called out for it, she wasn't actually sorry or regretful about her belief. That's what bothered me most—that someone I considered to be a close friend unconsciously saw me as unattractive. My skin tone was such a distraction for her that she analyzed *it* rather than my character or how I treated her as a friend. It made me feel like my dark skin was possibly creating a barrier between me and the people I loved, and maybe if I were lighter, my friend would like me more.

Although she was a woman of color herself, Carolina's proximity to whiteness affected what she considered to be beautiful. She was a lighter-skinned Mexican woman, my mom was a lighter-skinned Black woman, and that is what Western society has deemed acceptable and beautiful among non-white women. Unfortunately, as it is for many dark-skinned women, this wouldn't be the last time a close friend from my youth would express their aversion to my skin tone.

After a disagreement with a biracial friend in high school, completely unrelated to race or skin tone, she wrote "I am ugly and black" at the bottom of my homework assignment. Mind you, she was half-Black, raised by her white mother, and was very vocal about her dislike for her own hair texture. She was dealing with her own insecurities pertaining to her Blackness, and it made her feel better to know she didn't have full-on Black features like me. When she would criticize my Blackness, she was mostly speaking to color and not race. To her, I wasn't ugly *and* Black; I was ugly *because* my skin was black. Once again, it hurt deeply to realize that someone I admired and valued so much as a friend held negative views about my skin tone, so deeply that it was her immediate response to voice those opinions after the slightest disagreement. And then another friend, who is fully Black, slept at my house one night while my biracial cousin was staying over. This friend was maybe two to three shades lighter than me—and even trying to decide how many figurative shades lighter or darker someone is speaks to the absurdity of this exercise. While we were all in my bathroom, fixing our hair to go out to a movie, my friend asked my biracial cousin, "What does it feel like to be cousins with Bri? Like, someone who is so dark." I remember acting like I didn't have a problem with the question and then going into the next room to cry. It was as if my skin tone caused others, people I loved, to treat me like I was a social pariah. No matter the situation or topic, others always found ways to discuss my skin tone. It felt like the people in my life were so concerned with finding someone who served as an example of them not being the darkest in the room that they were willing to trade my self-esteem for it.

Colorism remains a huge issue in society, but there are professionals such as Dr. Sarah L. Webb who try to combat colorism by creating checklists that help people discern whether they have colorist views. Webb, a speaker, consultant, coach, and colorism expert, uses a ten-step checklist to determine if the people around you are colorists, and I found it to be tremendously helpful when weeding out the toxicity of colorism in my relationships. A person who is a colorist (1) explicitly expresses color-based dating preferences; (2) wishes to have light-skinned children; (3) makes jokes about skin color; (4) generally hyperfocuses on skin color and racialized features; (5) constantly and almost exclusively praises and affirms light skin or Eurocentric features, or people who have such features; (6) quickly and easily stereotypes or assumes negative things about dark-skinned people; (7) suggests that you or others would be so pretty if… ; (8) is paranoid about getting darker; (9) remains oblivious to, or gladly accepts, preferential treatment; and (10) is content with the oppression of dark-skinned people. Unfortunately, I was able to think of a friend or family member for every example. Embarrassingly, some of the examples even confirmed my own past experiences as a colorist, like naming other girls who were darker than me when I was ridiculed for having dark skin, to remove the attention from myself, or the period in high school when I thought I wanted to have mixed children and unknowingly was thinking that would make people respect me more. But it also made me think of examples of colorism within my own family. The majority of the men in my family seemed to date only light-skinned women. It was also common for my male family members to make "dark-skinned" jokes about one another during family reunions and gatherings. I remember hearing comments like "blue black" or "so dark that when you walk outside at night, only your teeth are visible." The problem with these "jokes" is that they aren't harmless at all, and when I was a child, witnessing this banter among adults, it signaled to me that my skin tone was not desirable, which erupted in me insecurities in how I saw myself.

Unsurprisingly, the examples of colorism I've detailed within my own family have been found to be true within other Black families. It isn't uncommon for some Black families to check the tips of a newborn baby's ears to see if their skin will get darker over time, or tell an interracial couple they'll have "pretty babies" (meaning babies with light skin, looser curls, and colored eyes—without even knowing what the child will actually look like), or hold lighter-skinned children to higher standards. A 2013 study exploring how parents assign roles, expectations, and acceptance to children based on their physical appearance looked at colorism as a basis for beauty. More specifically, the study found that "families displayed preferential treatment toward offspring based on skin tone and these differences varied by gender of child. Lighter skin daughters received higher quality parenting compared to those with darker skin." Other research suggests that parents of dark-skinned children may "scapegoat" them and hold their lighter-skinned children in higher regard, while other parents may provide more support to their darker-skinned children because they know that their child's skin tone could be viewed as a social disadvantage.

But not all first instances of colorism happen at home; in fact, most start at school. I met Mena, a thirty-year-old Sudanese woman, at a clothing launch party in New York City during the summer of 2021. I remember staring at her from across the large, crowded room, in awe of her flawless dark skin. Where she stood, the sun's glare from the windows reflected against her face, presenting an angelic glow. I just had to tell her that her skin was beautiful before the event was over. I'm sure she already knew, but I figured, like me, there was a time in her life when she had been told the opposite. I was right.

During an interview, I asked Mena to tell me about her earliest memory of being subjected to colorism.

> My family is from South Sudan and so we're known to be very dark-skinned. And so, my mom has dark skin and my dad has dark skin, so I never witnessed any negative discourse about dark skin at home. I moved to the US when I was about five years old, and I just remember some of the comments that kids would say about being dark-skinned. They would compare me to roaches and things like that. So by the age of like five, six years old, I was hyperaware that I was extremely dark-skinned. And then of course, outside of that, I started going to a Catholic school, which was predominantly white. So I was even made more aware of my deep dark skin complexion. Pretty much my entire childhood, it was always just in my face, as soon as I stepped outside of the door.

Despite attending a predominantly white Catholic school, it's little surprise that the kids who teased her most for having deep dark skin were other Black children:

> It mostly came from young Black boys. And if young Black girls were doing it, it was just to look cool in front of those Black guys. And a lot of these boys were definitely darker than me. So that was always confusing to me because we were almost the same complexion. I would kind of be like the butt of the joke with them. It was just so frustrating to be around. My confidence went down the drain. It was hard for me to look people straight in the eye for a while because I just wanted to kind of be invisible because I felt like if they saw me they would only see my dark skin. And at the time I had a really hard time accepting my deep complexion. I just didn't want to experience some of the things that I experienced anymore, so for a really long time, I just wouldn't look people in the eye.

When talking to Mena, I realized how closely her experience mirrored mine. Most of our bullies were from our own community, sometimes even the same complexion as us, and usually boys we liked. While colorism is something that people can experience far into adulthood, whether in dating, in the workplace, or just during day-to-day interactions, it's during childhood where it's often first introduced. Educational settings and other environments where children socialize—like a soccer team or the playground—are breeding grounds for colorism. Even college campuses have proven to be breeding grounds for discrimination based on skin tone. During the 1970s, African American fraternities and sororities used the "paper bag test" to differentiate between what was considered light skin and dark skin, in order to decide who would be allowed into their organization. What I find to be most hypocritical about this practice is its existence during a time when Black people were not allowed to join white fraternities and sororities, so they were left to create their own—yet carried out the same discrimination pushed on them by whites.

After learning about Mena's initial encounter with colorism, I was curious to know more, to see the other ways in which her experience might mirror my own. I asked Mena what was the most hurtful thing she had heard as a dark-skinned woman. She remembered the experience like it was yesterday. The tears I heard coming from the other side of the call suggested that for all the new appreciation she has for her skin tone now as an adult, the damage of colorism can still be long-lasting:

> I still remember this clear as day. I was like twelve, thirteen years old. I was hanging out with a bunch of friends and this boy named Mark Stevens—I still remember his name, still remember his face. We were all hanging out, and out of nowhere, he just looked at me because I was the darkest one there. He looked at me and went, 'Oh, she's just so ugly.' I said nothing to him in return. Instead, it just broke me. All I ever did

was be born with this skin tone and I can't do or
change anything about it. From then on, whenever
those guys would come to our neighborhood and hang
out, I would just completely avoid them. I wouldn't
hang out with them, just to avoid any bullying.

The bullying Mena experienced from her Black classmate
isn't uncommon among young, dark-skinned Black girls
throughout a lot of their grade school experience. In high
school, after tennis practice, I'd avoid crossing paths with any
of the football players who were heading home around the
same time as me. There had been too many encounters with
guys on the team, usually Black, who would see me heading
to my locker after spending two hours outdoors in the blazing
sun, sweaty and tanned from playing tennis, and make comments about me looking "rough" and "dark as hell." Each encounter made me less confident, ultimately pushing me to
break practice early or wait for them to pass by to dodge these
run-ins.

Another interviewee, a twenty-seven-year-old dark-skinned
woman, expressed a similar story about avoiding boys her age
when growing up, in order to dodge colorist remarks:

I went to a predominantly white, small Catholic high
school. I was the only dark-skinned girl in my school.
There were other Black girls, but they were either

mixed-race or they were lighter-skinned. So whenever I would have to take the city bus home from school, I remember dreading whenever we'd get to a certain point and we'd have to pick up kids from this public school. I mean, those guys were so fine. And I had crushes on a whole bunch of them from a distance, but being faced with them on the bus was so scary for me. I remember one time they got on the bus and I literally wanted to just die in my seat. They would come, sit in the back of the bus, and you know they're talking about you, and they'd make comments about my skin tone and my hair too. If I had a natural hairstyle or something, they would make fun of that. And I have fuller lips, so they would make comments about that. But what killed me is that these are the same guys who would go after white girls in my school and they would make comments like, 'Oh, she's not white-white. She has that olive skin tone, and she has fuller lips,' and praising these white girls for features that are completely standard and common in our community.

On TikTok, stories like this from young Black women detailing their negative experiences with colorism from members of their own race consistently go viral. I didn't have to look long before discovering a trend where a Black woman, @priscillakarikarii, asks other Black women to tell her what the most disrespectful thing a Black guy has ever said to them as a Black woman. I instantly noticed that the majority of these videos featured dark-skinned Black women with stories of colorism. One user, @morgantheblackfairy, detailed a heartbreaking story about an encounter she had with a Black man who asked for her phone number. After giving the guy her number, Morgan told him she would prefer they get to know each other in person rather than texting all the time. One time, when they met up, the guy made her feel uncomfortable by coming on to her too strongly, so she ended all contact with him. To this boundary, the guy responded, "You're just dark and ugly," and further told her that he was using her because dark-skinned girls always give sex easily. According to Morgan, the guy, who is darker than her, then said, "I would never get with a tar baby like you." At the end of the sixty-second clip, you can see Morgan's expression change, suggesting that revisiting the incident was traumatic and painful. But like Morgan's, and those of so many other dark-skinned women, these stories that we work so hard to bury never really leave us. What was even more unsettling is that she mentioned there are numerous negative stories she has like these, and that choosing one story over the others was challenging. As Morgan said, the situation had a profound effect on her self-esteem, speaking largely to the emotional and psychological weight these cruel and harmful words have on dark-skinned women over the long term.

Before the rise of social media movements that created public transparency and discourse around these issues, stories like these were shameful and embarrassing to recount to anyone. Now, however, the numerous public anecdotes detailing situations of colorism where dark-skinned women are the victims are popular, and this has made it less acceptable to blatantly be a colorist online. It wasn't always that way.

I joined Twitter in 2009, during the summer before entering my freshman year of high school. My first encounters with being on the app were filled with anti-Black, misogynoir, and colorist tweets that would push me into a dark slump of self-hatred and fear. Vile tweets about Black women, especially dark-skinned Black women, consumed my timeline. Boys and grown men would often joke about having sex with a dark-skinned Black woman as if it was something disgusting or easy to do. There was one particular trend that first made me question my body and whether my private parts were abnormal or something that I should be ashamed of. Images of sliced roast beef to signify a dark-skinned woman's vagina spread among my online community almost daily and became a joke among, mostly, the Black kids in my school. But colorism online didn't cease with desirability politics. In more severe cases, violent posts claiming that dark-skinned Black women were promiscuous and "easy" to sleep with and should be physically abused, raped, and killed infiltrated my feed. But it wasn't just boys and men who took part in our destruction online. Many lighter Black women chose silence or played along because our public marginalization simultaneously elevated them. My Twitter timeline started to feel like a battlefield of people competing for who could say the most disrespectful thing about us. The only way to completely avoid seeing these tweets would mean not being online at all, which at the time seemed unrealistic for someone in high school.

In an op-ed titled "How Colourism and Misogynoir Affected a Generation of Dark-Skinned Black Women On and Off the Timeline," writer Tobi Kyeremateng recalled her experience dealing with colorism on Twitter between 2009 and 2012, while growing up in South London. Her gruesome experience speaks to the internet's ability to spread dangerous rhetoric across borders. She writes,

> The dehumanisation and animalisation of black women's bodies gave room for adolescent black girls to question the normality of our features. Noting that these comments were coming from black boys and men feels uncomfortable, but the swelling heap of abuse black girls and women suffered is an uncomfortable fact we have to sit with. Alongside black boys and men, black girls and women become complicit in a culture of anti-black and colourist rhetoric. In short, black communities became agents of perpetuating harmful white supremacist ideologies against ourselves online. This internalized anti-blackness would hold storage in my body like a virus for the next decade to come, infecting my self-esteem and leading to the progression of anxiety, depression and body dysmorphia. I wouldn't be the only one.... I have seen many black women over the years remind us of the black men who had built their large followings on the backs of the black women

they had slandered back in the day while being gaslit
into thinking that era of Twitter was a pure blip. Over a
decade later, we stand to face the same issues.

Negative comments about Black women's hair, bodies, and
choices are still rampant online, but social media also provides us with a plethora of images of beautiful dark-skinned
women, images of dark-skinned women being loved and
courted, and gives us a platform to call out colorism collectively, with the support of other women. In the "How Social
Media Has Helped Black Women Reclaim Their Beauty" episode of *Dark Girls 2*, a documentary that explores the preju-
dices darker-skinned women face around the world, different
dark-skinned women pay homage to social media as a tool to
deal with colorism. By following pages that celebrate the
beauty of dark skin, dark-skinned models, and dark-skinned
women living their best lives, dark-skinned women all around
the world are able to find representation online, even when
the outside world does not frequently make space for it. One
woman in the documentary shared,

> Social media is a great way to physically put
> something in front of you that can be a constant
> encouragement. On my Instagram, I follow things
> that encourage me, and I follow, visually, people that
> look like me or people that are in places that I want
> to be, and they're Black people. And I think it's
> important to put that in front of your face because it's
> an encouragement. But we didn't have that even ten

years ago. So now I feel like a younger generation can now look and know and celebrate those things on a regular basis in a way that I couldn't, when I was first starting.

Like racism, colorism is rooted in ignorance and follows the same ideology of systematic and verbal oppression. It leaves dark-skinned women out of business opportunities, and it welcomes harmful stereotypes about women, suggesting that dark-skinned women are aggressive and masculine, which results in us being treated as such. It wounds self-esteem and self-worth, which has a direct correlation to depression, and it makes us more susceptible to rape and assault because it is assumed that we are hypersexual beings or a breeding ground for violence. It disables us mentally, emotionally, and spiritually and, as a result, pushes some of us to disengage entirely from certain members of our race. And furthermore, by separating us into distinctive tiers based solely on phenotypic traits, it weakens our community overall. And that's exactly what white supremacy wants.

It's important when talking about colorism to acknowledge its history. Colorism stems directly from racism; therefore, it's a tactic employed by white people to create division within the Black community as well as justify harm to the Black community. For example, in the case of O. J. Simpson, *Time* magazine's front cover showcased a drastically darkened image of

Simpson, which many criticized as an attempt to display him as guilty. The association of darker skin with danger, violence, and guilt exists because of the idea that lighter skin is close to white skin. It also represents white ancestry and therefore is employed to create a stark contrast regarding innocence between Black and white people. As long as we continue to associate dark skin with guilt, crime, and even unattractiveness, white skin will be perceived as the opposite of that. I believe that if Black people keep this fundamental fact at top of mind—that colorism is racism's younger sister—we'll be more conscious of the ways in which we uphold the practice. We'll also be more aware of the ways in which the practice is upheld in our systems, and not just dating, the entertainment industry, and bullying from other kids.

While I was growing up, colorism planted its hand in everything I consumed and everything I loved. Besides R & B beauties like Brandy and Kelly Rowland, I rarely saw mainstream female musicians who looked like me. And in the films I loved, if any young Black women were present at all, the dark-skinned women never played the romantic, desirable lead. Instead they were the loud, annoying, unattractive best friend. And as I reached my twenties, not much had changed.

In *High Fidelity*, one of my favorite shows to hit Hulu in 2020, the lead, Rob, is played by Zoë Kravitz, whom I'm a huge fan of, but who does not represent me at all. She's biracial with fine hair, very light skin, and soft features. She fits the image that Hollywood deems acceptable when the character is a Black woman, and her dark-skinned, fat best friend, Cherise, played by Da'Vine Joy Randolph, fits the stereotype of the undesirable side character. While Kravitz's character experiments with different relationships, attracting both men and women of various racial backgrounds, Randolph's character is rejected in the few instances we see her attempt to flirt at all. She's portrayed as asexual, she's the only main character who doesn't have her own storyline, and her personality is childish and annoying to the point that viewers cringe at some of her lines. Yet, she supports Kravitz's character while she forces herself into relationship drama and infidelity. Despite my disappointment in the show's character development, I binged the entire season in two days. All my friends were watching it, and there was no way I would miss out on the female spinoff of the 2000 classic starring John Cusack and Kravitz's own mother, Lisa Bonet. In all my excitement and love for the show, I knew minutes into the first episode what each character's personality would be like throughout the entire season. I knew who would have a love life and who would never be seen kissing someone. The roles of Rob and Cherise played on the repeated tropes Hollywood affords its Black female characters in that the light-skinned character was worthy of love and the dark-skinned character displayed an asexual nature. The light-skinned character is allowed to be soft and have depth, while the dark-skinned character isn't fleshed out and relies overmuch on stereotypical sassy-ness.

Honestly, I could have written the script myself, because colorism has a way of making everything in television and film feel identical. It speaks not only to the lack of creativity and the abundance of ignorance of the TV writers and producers who breathe life into these characters, but also to the dullness colorism generates. Maybe that's why I wasn't too disappointed when news broke that the show would not be renewed for a second season.

My friends and I felt a similar flatness when the actors for the *Gossip Girl* reboot were announced. The original series debuted in 2007 and lacked any diversity among the main cast, but it was the early 2000s, so no one really expected diversity anyway. But in 2021, after a decade of dark-skinned women in Hollywood taking to social media to demand more (and better) representation, the modern reboot still failed to cast any Black women who aren't light-skinned. In fact, all three of the Black women chosen for lead roles appear biracial or light-skinned, highlighting the ways in which Hollywood continuously favors light skin tones when it comes to Black woman leads. This time around, I wasn't interested in the show at all.

Similar to how society has grown somewhat bored with seeing white singles find love, year after year, on *The Bachelor*, some dark-skinned Black women are fatigued by the constant push for only light-skinned women in positive, leading Black roles. What biases do these producers and casting directors hold that prevent them from casting and writing dark-skinned Black women who have depth, who are capable of love? All of this sheds light on the ways in which Black women aren't invited into writers' rooms or given other opportunities to flesh out and bring authentic life into these characters and stories.

In the '90s, there was a dearth of Black shows to choose from, but with the exception of *Moesha* and *The Jamie Foxx Show*, colorism was still highly reinforced in the casting of female leads. Growing up, I consumed a mix of white and Black shows. *The Fresh Prince of Bel-Air*, *Martin*, and *Sister, Sister* were a few of the classics my brother would force me to watch with him after dinner. In *The Fresh Prince of Bel-Air*, I first developed the idea that light-skinned women are inherently nicer than dark-skinned women when the original Aunt Viv character, a dark-skinned woman (Janet Hubert), was replaced during the third season with a much lighter actress (Daphne Maxwell Reid). Along with the change in skin tone came a more obvious change in character. The new Aunt Vivian was more gentle in her disciplinary approach, had a softer tone of voice, and lacked the edge and "take charge" attitude of her predecessor. This was a mindless fumble by the creators of the show, who failed to maintain the role's character. Perhaps skin tone outweighed common practice when casting changes occurred, like casting someone who looks similar to the previous actor, or at least acts the same. In the 2022 *Fresh Prince* reboot, the critiques have been addressed, with the latest Aunt Viv holding a noticeably more prominent role and being of darker complexion.

When I watched *Martin*, I first started to idolize light-skinned women as romantics and disassociate attractiveness from dark-skinned women. When Martin lays eyes on Gina, it's as if he's never seen a woman more beautiful. He admires her, then pursues her, then courts her, eventually marrying her later in the series. It's the way love is supposed to look, and it inspired my young mind to look for that same treatment from men when I got older. It also taught me how not to act, if you wanted men to find you attractive, specifically with Pam's role. Played by Tichina Arnold, Pam is the dark-skinned best friend of Gina. She's extremely loud, sassy, and explosive, and she always has something to complain about. Oftentimes she argues with Martin, and Gina steps in as the soft, rational mediator. As for Pam's love life, it's almost nonexistent. She occasionally flirts with a guy on the show named Tommy, and they have a brief relationship, but it comes to an end by the next season and the two remain just friends. The only other time someone took an interest in Pam was during the first season, and she often responded to his advances by nonsensically losing her temper with him. Twenty-eight years apart, Pam's role in *Martin* highly reflected Cherise's role in *High Fidelity*.

Watching the differences between light-skinned and dark-skinned characters during my adolescence had a huge impact on how I viewed dark-skinned women, and therefore myself. I rarely witnessed us being loved, or even wanting love. Love seemed to be reserved for lighter women. Black love itself is already portrayed as an anomaly. There are Instagram pages and Tumblr accounts dedicated to showing it off and just proving that it exists and is attainable. But these pages, like the TV and film I've consumed, less often showcase Black love that I can see for myself. I'm not saying that love between a light-skinned woman and a dark-skinned man does not count as Black love, but it is the only Black love pushed on us so heavily, and after some time, those who fit the description begin to manifest only that kind of pairing. In some cases, it can make you wonder how easily attainable Black love is for you, with colorism infiltrating the pursuit.

Even the shows with characters closer to my age did very little to represent girls who looked like me. No one wanted to be Dijonay in *The Proud Family*, but everyone wished to emulate Penny or have the lifestyle of LaCienega. There were no dark-skinned Black girls to even wish to emulate, whether it was *That's So Raven*, *Shake It Up*, or *Cory in the House*. Besides Keke Palmer, there weren't any girls who looked like me who played roles I could compare myself to. Being a young dark-skinned millennial Black girl meant mostly only seeing white and light-skinned girls on the majority of kids' shows, suggesting that something was wrong with our skin and constructing this unconscious attraction to lighter skin.

Optimistically, some members of Hollywood are committed to painting new, positive narratives around dark-skinned women. In *Insecure*, Issa Rae and Yvonne Orji played Issa and Molly, two dark-skinned beautiful young women who navigate a vibrant dating life and climb up their individual corporate ladders. They are lead characters, they experience being loved and courted by men, and they're successful in their respective lines of work. Their roles portray a realistic, non-stereotypical version of dark-skinned Black women, as opposed to the excessively loud, ignorant, and uneducated trope Hollywood has pushed for decades. Shows like these, where dark-skinned women made the media they wanted to see and were able to hold on to creative control, therefore were able to promote the perception of dark-skinned women as loveable romantic partners.

Without proper representation when I was a child, it felt impossible to find reasons to believe my dark skin could possibly be beautiful. It took me twenty-one years to finally accept, appreciate, and then love my skin. In conversation with my friends, I've come to realize the power of my communities, both online and offline, that have contributed to the self-love and self-appreciation I've developed during my twenties. Through online communities of young Black women, specifically dark-skinned Black women, I have found solidarity in my past struggles and have started to truly love and admire my skin. And while there is still a ways to go for people of all shades to support a better life for dark-skinned women, I am confident knowing that we have platforms to create the experiences we have not been afforded in the past.

CHAPTER 4

The Not-So-Token Black Friend

My earliest memory of a guy I liked telling me that I was pretty was in the tenth grade. Gabriel and I had attended the same private Catholic elementary and middle school when we were younger. He ended up attending the private Catholic high school that I was meant to feed into. But because my parents, understandably, couldn't afford to keep paying thousands of dollars a year for the tuition, Gabriel and I went our separate ways. Although my new school was in a different city and district, I stayed in touch, mostly online, with all of my close friends from St. Rose of Lima. Including Gabriel.

During my sophomore year, my dad surprised me with a car on my sixteenth birthday. It wasn't brand-new, but it was a black two-door Chevy Cobalt—easily mistaken for a more expensive sports car. Having my own vehicle made it easy for me to visit my friends from my old school. I would often attend their football and basketball games and quickly became known as "the girl from the public school." I had street knowledge and dabbled in "controversial" experiences like attending a series of popular house parties thrown by two college guys and hanging out late with older high schoolers from "bad" schools. Also, I was coming into my own, growing into my features, and I'd finally started to dress attractively. To my friends still in Catholic school, I seemed cool, different, interesting, because I wasn't confined to this private school bubble. And Gabriel noticed it too.

One evening, I attended a basketball game with my friend Carson, who was a junior at the school. Gabriel approached us, after months of liking my photos on Instagram, and embraced me in a hug. "I can't believe you're here," he said, sounding so surprised, even though he had seen me at previous games. I guess he had finally worked up the courage to greet me. I laughed and told him that it was nice to see him again. We exchanged numbers, and then a week later I was sitting in the back seat of his mom's SUV after he had taken me out to dinner. "You're so pretty for a Black girl," he told me, right before pulling me in for a kiss. At the time, I was elated by his comment. It made me feel attractive and, shamefully, better than the other Black girls we knew. Gabriel, this popular, wealthy, non-Black guy, had chosen me. I made the cut. And that itself made me feel pretty, even if just for a Black girl.

Now that I'm wiser, it's shameful to have felt pride at this backhanded comment, which eventually would become so common during my encounters with my non-Black peers. Throughout my time in high school, this comment came up pretty often. A white guy on the baseball team whom I had flirted with from time to time told me he thought I was the prettiest Black girl at our school. A light-skinned Black guy who wanted to take my virginity told me he would only sleep with me because I was pretty for a dark-skinned girl. A foreign exchange student from Finland, whom everyone in my class had a crush on, told another guy that he thought I was cute for a Black girl, before friending me on Facebook.

I would never describe myself as a token Black woman, but these compliments, or, more accurately, microaggression statements disguised as admiration, meant I was a token, even without trying. My looks, and probably my tone of voice, and even having a nice car and a large house, made me palatable to white people and other people who held biases against Black people and, more specifically, dark-skinned Black women. The combination of my suburban affect and the class level of my family made my peers feel like I was respectable in a way that transcended Black people. They didn't associate being cool or pretty with dark-skinned women unless there was something that seemed extraordinary about us. And then there are ways in which I *had* actually tokenized myself. Since grade school—the first experience I had that involved interacting with people outside of my community—the role of being a token was placed on me and later became something I unconsciously perpetuated. But because of my young age and the naivety that follows from living under your parents' guidance, it seems more appropriate to refer to this particular tokenizing period as assimilating, or social survival. The city I lived in was predominantly Black, which meant the local soccer team I played for, the Girl Scout group I joined, and the church I attended were all predominantly Black. Our neighborhood was as suburban as suburban could get. Sprawling lawns and rows of similarly constructed large houses, if not the huge luxury SUVs parked in every driveway, signaled the middle class. Signs that rooted for our local high school's football and basketball teams were present in every yard, showcasing the pride my neighbors held for our city. At times, DeSoto, Texas, felt like a Black utopia, but to outsiders, it was perceived as the hood, a place that was ghetto, sometimes dangerous, and lacking in affluence.

When my parents enrolled me in that prestigious Catholic school near a wealthy, white Dallas neighborhood, I grew embarrassed at being from a Black suburban city. I remember attending birthday parties at the homes of some of my friends and feeling like my three-bedroom home could not compare. Sometimes I would even lie to some of my classmates and tell them I lived in the same neighborhood as them. Like many other non-white kids growing up in an ethnic household but attending a predominantly white school, I did anything in my power to fit in with my rich, popular, white counterparts. I begged my mother to let me get my hair straightened professionally, as opposed to styling it at home, so it would appear flowy. Even some of the hairstylists I went to aided my assimilation, suggesting to my mom and me that I *needed* a relaxer because my hair was "unmanageable."

By my last year of elementary school, I was enrolled in public school because, as mentioned, the cost of private school was becoming unaffordable for my parents. Instead of sending me to the local elementary school in our city, I attended a DeSoto school for one year and then transferred to the school district where my father worked as an educator. This school district had a more positive reputation than that of the one in my city, and my dad worked there, so my parents figured this would be a smoother transition from the private education I had during most of my elementary school career. I continued attending schools in this district all the way through high school. Although I now had an opportunity to make more Black friends through school, which I did, I found myself still trying to fit in with the popular white kids too. After all, it's what I was accustomed to. I adopted the suburban vernacular of my white schoolmates and shopped at beachy clothing stores like Hollister and Abercrombie, with the hope that my well-off white friends would assume I, too, had money. I was often told things like "you talk like a white person" or "you act like a white girl." Weirdly, I felt accepted and similar to them, and therefore I was less teased than my Black friends who chose not to engage with our white peers so intimately.

During my senior year of high school, when I competed in a Black beauty pageant in Texas, I felt connected to my authentic self for the first time. After all, I was surrounded by numerous young Black women, of all shades and hair textures, being judged on our beauty—beauty made possible by melanin and feature variety and kinks and coils. There were no blond girls for me to compare myself to, or redheaded girls who were considered more "diverse" than the rest. Thinness wasn't the basis of beauty, and the onstage question portion focused on how you would be a role model to younger Black girls, instead of what makes you different from the other girls competing. The judges were mostly Black women, an instant comfort for me because I knew their beauty standards were not based on proximity to Western European standards. Unlike my experience with modeling, being around girls I felt comfortable with made all the difference. Backstage, we listened to R & B and hip-hop music while our makeup artists prepped our faces for the show. We borrowed one another's foundation and traded lipsticks, because the shades complemented our skin tones. Some girls sported braids, while others rocked their natural Afros. The space was unapologetically Black.

That evening, I took home a crown for the beauty division, and the view I held of myself had been altered for life. It was the first time I truly felt beautiful as a Black woman. But not as a Black woman with softer features or a modelesque stature, as I had so often been told was what defined my beauty— but as a dark-skinned, full-lipped Black woman with tightly coiled hair.

When I got to college, almost instantly I dropped the assimilation act because it no longer felt like an obligation to make friends. After rushing a predominantly white spirit group (which is basically a non-Greek sorority) and attending a few house parties where I was one of the only Black people in attendance, I found myself becoming hyperaware of my Blackness and, as a result, disinterested in white college culture. Shotgunning beers, rapping along to hip-hop songs without knowing at all what the lyrical content is about, making out with random people at a party, sharing drinks, and popping Adderall before a night out was immensely unappealing to me. I was beginning to feel hypervisible at these gatherings—not because I was one of the few Black people, but because of how much I didn't fit in, and didn't care to fit in.

During one party, a group of white fraternity guys who took interest in me approached me by telling me they like Gucci Mane and Young Thug. That was their icebreaker— mentioning two prominent Black hip-hop artists who weren't even playing at the party. I responded by telling them that was cool, because I didn't want to draw attention to myself in this space. At another party, "My Nigga" by YG came on the sound system, and the white partygoers pointed to their Black token friends every time the chorus spewed "my nigga, my nigga" while mouthing the words. Of course this was problematic, but even more, it revealed that so many of the white people I surrounded myself with struggled to socialize with people outside of their race without calling attention to the fact that their friends were not white. Their ignorance coupled with their microaggression statements, their biases, and the stereotypes they place on people like me affected the way they interact with Black people interpersonally and, most importantly, made me see these people in a way that grade school had never revealed. Also, I *was* in college now. There were more Black students in my classes, some of my professors were Black, and there were specific groups, sororities, and spaces created for us to freely and safely exist. I didn't need to conform anymore because my survival no longer depended on it.

In grade school, it sometimes felt like I had no choice. It was expected for Black people to assimilate in order to make friends and be teased less. But over time, I realized assimilating just got me through. It didn't save me from microaggressions, uncomfortable situations, or being singled out. Any Black person surrounding themselves with a predominantly white group or attending a predominantly white school is going to experience some kind of mistreatment at some point, whether it be subtle or blatant. But in college, my social circle quickly became mostly Black and brown, and there was less of a need to assimilate to any specific standards in order to be perceived as a respectable person. I felt a sense of relief when I identified the parts of campus that Black students adopted as their own, the parties thrown by Black fraternities and sororities, the probates where you could turn up and be unapologetically Black, the lunch halls where I could flirt with the Black athletes, and the Black studies classes instructed by Black professors. My group of Black girlfriends were all from various parts of the country, yet we all had similar experiences with conforming in grade school. By our junior year, we all decided to transition our hair from relaxed to natural, a scary change for most of us, but made easier when done together.

When I graduated college and entered corporate America, I found myself forced to assimilate to white standards once again. I quickly learned that I needed to be *that* Black girl, whom my white coworkers not only admired but felt comfortable around. That meant not being too loud in the office but being loud enough to make them think I was funny rather than unfriendly. It meant not twerking at the holiday party but hyping up my white coworkers who would attempt to twerk anytime a hip-hop song was played. I haven't seen a single episode of *The Office* or learned the full lyrics to any ABBA song, but anytime either relic of white pop culture was mentioned at work, I knew to laugh along and appear amused. What was once a practice that I had buried after a semester of college resurfaced as a frustrating facade used to advocate for a raise, a promotion, and social acceptance at work. What made it worse is that I didn't particularly want the approval of my coworkers in the same way I longed to be accepted by my schoolmates when I was younger. Personally, I felt I didn't have nearly as much in common with my white coworkers as I did with the Black friends I had made at work, but their approval was necessary in order to succeed in a white-dominant office environment. So, I conformed to appease them, and in almost every situation, it still had very little effect on my success at any media company I worked for. I think that's what many white people fail to realize when they recruit Black people to their company in order to uphold their self-proclaimed liberal agenda. They're not necessarily seeking Black culture or Black identity when hiring us; they're seeking a head count, a box to check, something to symbolize their progressiveness. In wanting diversity but not the diverse cultures or perspectives attached to that diverse hire, white and non-Black people who employ Black people unknowingly push us to conform to their standards, lifestyle, and customs. In this process, we mask our Blackness and minimize our presence in the office by wearing white-approved hairstyles, dressing in Westernized clothing, adapting avoidant behavioral traits, and code-switching.

Code-switching is defined as alternating between two or more varieties of language in conversation, but for Black people, it's more than a linguistic practice, it's a survival mechanism and learned behavior mostly introduced during our youth. It combats biases held against us as children in grade school and as adults when we have to plead with the police or other authority figures—but only to some extent. It's a practice a Black person oftentimes cannot advance without in corporate America, but rarely does it set us above or even equal to our white colleagues. Oftentimes, code-switching opens the door to a room that we were never meant to be in, it gauges interest in a topic we weren't expected to know anything about, it grants us a chance, but still not a fair one.

What might appear simple—to switch our natural expression on and off—is a frustrating and stressful practice that quite frequently leaves members of marginalized groups feeling inauthentic and disappointed in themselves. When you navigate your day-to-day interactions by tapping in and out of your true self, and dancing between two separate worlds, not only is your mental energy continuously drained, but your self-confidence suffers from knowing that people are accepting you only because you're presenting a watered-down version of yourself. Freedom of expression is known to create joy for people across ethnic groups and gender identities, but Black women often are not allowed to partake in this luxury unless they are in predominantly Black female spaces. It comes as no surprise that research on code-switching has found that the survival tactic mostly occurs "in spaces where negative stereotypes of Black people run counter to what are considered 'appropriate' behaviors and norms for a specific environment." Whether it be adjusting one's style of speech, appearance, behavior, or expression, many of the Black women I spoke with noted that code-switching benefits white people and not the Black code-switcher. While it creates a more comfortable environment for the recipients, rarely does it result in fair treatment, quality service, less preconceived judgment, and employment opportunities for the code-switchers. As Black women, we've been taught that these practices will result in corporate and social success in white-dominant environments, but through personal experience, I've come to realize that masking my Blackness has done very little to help me thrive in mainstream culture or in corporate America.

In my early career, I quickly became aware of the ways in which white office-culture norms could negatively affect my career projection. During a performance review with a previous manager, I was critiqued for not socializing with my teammates, or as he put it, not embedding myself with my coworkers. Ultimately, my manager expressed that I wasn't someone who worked well in team settings, and that I possibly wasn't a good fit for the team, simply because I chose not to socialize with my coworkers beyond what was required of me to do my job. Because my chance at a promotion or raise was based solely on these reviews, it was imperative to question his assessment, so I asked for further explanation. I remember feeling his hesitation about even meeting with me when I reached out to him to discuss the review. I felt indignation toward him for being so resistant to my desire to address his feedback. "If you couldn't stand by what you submitted, then why submit it all?" I thought. So I pressed him, demanding that we meet about it in person rather than having me send questions and concerns to him via Slack.

I felt that my manager was always discomfited by my presence, but this became even more apparent whenever our meetings took place. He'd appear anxious when we chatted, even in passing, which was not how I had seen him interact with my non-Black teammates. In a meeting about my performance, I asked my boss to give me a few examples of how

I was not acting as a team player, and he flinched. It was in this conversation that I realized his broad feedback stemmed from his disapproval of me not being active in our team's private Slack channel, which, mind you, existed solely for sending memes, making jokes, and talking about funny tweets. In regard to our Slack channel dedicated to work-related manners, I kept notifications on and always responded in a timely manner. My boss also criticized my "disinterest" in being embedded in the team because I often passed on team events, like going out for drinks and movie nights, none of which were mandatory.

Ultimately, my boss never had any valid examples that were connected to my actual work. And I made this known to him in the meeting. I told him that my disinterest in building friendships outside of work with my coworkers does not equate to me not being a team player. I went on to explain to him what makes someone a team player and gave him examples of how I do embody a team player. I was a reliable coworker who always met my deadlines and communicated when I would be away from work far in advance. Lastly, I told him that I did not appreciate his personal negative feelings toward me affecting my career advancement at the company. He struggled to respond to this, which I assume was because no one had ever called out the ways in which he may have allowed his own internalized biases, informed by his whiteness, to hinder his ability to properly manage a team. It's also important to mention that I was the only Black person on staff, and the only person of color at all on this team, other than our interns. This predicament isn't uncommon in work settings where unfair performance reviews based on being a "team player," or more so, being someone highly acquainted with their coworkers, are given to Black employees who are on predominantly non-Black teams. The idea that someone is a good worker as long as they are a good fit—more specifically, someone who fits in—is a culturally white office practice that only benefits the majority. I personally don't think my manager intended to harm me or belittle my performance when he made these unfair assessments—I think he was conditioned to manage this way.

Unlike blue-collar jobs like retail and the service industry, which rely on subservience, corporate America, and especially media and tech companies, thrive on socializing and networking. The who-you-know adage, sometimes trumping hard work, is a skill that many Black people have to develop to fit into these environments because this type of socialization at work doesn't come naturally to us. Predominantly white work environments are rarely inviting to diversity and instead are spaces that a lot of us do not feel comfortable forming real relationships in, forcing us to alter our presentation. For my coworkers, their whiteness prevented them from realizing that while not engaging daily in non-work-related matters, I was doing the job I was hired to do. But all that mattered was my disinterest in their personal lives, and my nonexistent desire to befriend them made them uncomfortable with my presence.

When I expressed this issue to my boss, who was writing my reviews, he wouldn't agree with me. Maybe because that would mean admitting his judgment of me was skewed.

This lack of taking responsibility was a common practice among the white employees at this company when called out for any mistake they made. My boss at the time told me that working well in a team was as important as getting my work done, completely bypassing the reality that my choice to not send memes all day or talk about shows that I didn't watch held no relation to my ability to work with other people. When I shared my experience on Twitter of being penalized for my "introverted" behavior at my past media job, thousands of other Black women, who are all too familiar with being on the receiving end of gaslighting in work environments, responded. Their similar experiences validated the common realities we face:

> It doesn't matter if you're introverted or extraverted, there's always a reason why high-performing Black women get negative reviews. I'm in between. I engaged very well, am a top performer in my department, and often chosen for projects with high visibility customers. Execs would tell me how clients raved about me and always requested I be sent to meet and work with them onsite. But because I'm actually funny and charismatic, they'd pass on me for promotions because it's not considered professional to joke with coworkers. Yet, they kept putting me out there with clients.

Black women aren't allowed to be [insert any adjective in dictionary]. I've had performance reviews that rated me "needs improvement" because I was "too quiet," "too independent," "not a team player," and my all time fave "too serious." It's all coded for too BLACK.

The issue is that there's usually only one of us in the space and they are uncomfortable if we're not being their best friend. If we do the work we're hired to do, our social interactions are our choice and not a reflection of my ability to do the job.

This gets to the heart of why racial problems persist. I bet most of those white folk have never been in a truly foreign environment and can't understand how unsafe it feels—so they misinterpret caution as rejection. That on top of white guilt is a toxic stew.

After two years of employment, I was let go from the company during a massive layoff. While human resources reps insist the decisions were "random" (losing your job without notice or suspicion is unfortunately common practice in the media industry), my white coworker of the same position, who became a full-time employee after I did, and was close friends with my boss and other members of the team, was saved from the cuts. It's hard not to question whether her fitting in more with the company's culture played a role in her continued employment and if my battle with ludicrous and unconscious biases ended mine. This experience definitely opened my eyes to the realization that white people have to work less to be a culture fit. Their upbringing and culture are already accepted in the workplace so they do not have to adjust; they simply get to exist. It doesn't matter whether they're an introvert or an extrovert, outgoing and loud, or reserved and timid—any character they wish to take on is perceived as natural to them and worthy of acceptance. They get to be multidimensional and don't have to work as hard to appeal to others. But Black women have to live between certain margins and can't overstep certain lines, because when we act like ourselves, it's perceived as a threat to whiteness, white professional and social norms, and white power structures.

On top of code-switching, there is an unrealistic expectation that Black women are expected to handle more work because it's already assumed that we will be lazy workers if we are not constantly challenged. Another job I held was for a small public relations startup where I was the only Black person, and person of color, employed during my time there. During the interview process, my boss was enthusiastic about my previous work experience and knowledge of inclusive marketing. Shortly after being brought on, and taking on work outside my scope, I was let go when I failed to run and manage more than seven social media accounts for various clients. Early on I recognized that the job was meant for a team—just glancing at the business structure of any other company's social media department would prove that one person cannot manage multiple social media accounts on their own. So I asked my boss for support once I realized the number of social accounts kept increasing, but my boss didn't prioritize my request.

However, when other members of the team expressed that they needed support in running numerous PR accounts, their needs were immediately met by hiring interns. The expectation that I should be able to not only manage but excel in running multiple social media accounts without any help put me in an impossible position to succeed. As my workload increased, my pay did not, and taking time off for vacation or even a dentist appointment meant my work for the day would fall short—as I had no backup on my team to take over my duties. I accepted that I would most likely be laid off soon and started to search for new work until that day came. After all, as I had learned at my previous job, Black women rarely are heard or believed when they ask for support or make a case for themselves. Six months into the position, I was fired midday and asked to pack up my belongings in front of my coworkers. I wasn't upset. I was prepared and knew that this mistreatment was completely out of my control. Code-switching, straightening my hair, and dressing in business casual attire only got me in the door with this company but did very little to earn me respect or support during my employment.

According to *Harvard Business Review*, "Expressing shared interests with members of dominant groups promotes similarity with powerful organizational members, which raises the chance of promotions because individuals tend to affiliate with people they perceive as similar." But in my case, and the cases of my peers, conforming to white office culture has never protected our jobs, and instead has resulted in high stress levels and repeated disappointment. Appealing to my white boss and colleagues did not result in support when I asked for it, despite my white colleagues receiving support instantly when they expressed needing help. The stereotypes that Black women are lazy workers and complain too much outweighed my Banana Republic office attire and soft-spoken articulation. And while my boss would never consider herself racist or implicitly biased, her actions toward me spoke differently than how she believed herself to be. In these recurring instances of dealing with white bosses who were biased toward their employees but publicly portrayed themselves as welcoming people, I became aware of how some white people believe they are accepting of Black people because of the support they offer to Black people they don't know, Black people they don't interact with every day, Black people they don't even have to converse with. Maybe they've donated to an organization that supports Black businesses, or they voted for Black politicians, but in their daily interactions, they are unconsciously treating the Black people in their life unfairly. How many of them can say that the Black people who know them personally would endorse their progressive-liberal character?

My greatest realization from working under white bosses who claim to value diverse perspectives and build inclusive teams is that I was always expected to cater to their customs and beliefs but never received the same respect. At least not until my suggestions, beliefs, and ideas were expressed largely by other white people. Once Black Lives Matter infiltrated news feeds during summer 2020, many of my white colleagues from my first media job adopted "woke" personas online. It's interesting, but not surprising, to see my ex-colleagues parade their support for the Black community on their Twitter and Instagram accounts when I remember the numerous times they would reject any conversations centering race or white privilege when I would enter the Slack channel. Additionally, it's frustrating to witness these former colleagues so loudly claim to be welcoming allies when I recall them creating a living hell of a work environment for the only Black person on their team due to cultural differences. The PR company that I was laid off from also recently rebranded its goals and values after seeing other white-led companies do the same after summer 2020. The majority of the recommendations I suggested to create a more inclusive company had been instilled shortly after the racial reckoning, such as hiring more people of color, donating to a campaign that supports marginalized communities, and being vocal about racism on the company's social media accounts. Yet, months before the racial reckoning, it was these suggestions, coupled with asking for support, that separated me from my coworkers and pushed my boss to oppose me. I was the Black girl who was becoming "too Black" for the company culture. I wasn't afraid to critique our company and call out its blind spots. Through pushing my progressive agenda and suggesting solutions to the company's weaknesses—everything I mentioned I would do in my first interview—I was shunned and caused discomfort for my white "open-minded" bosses. So I was dropped after continuously advocating for myself and demanding support. My bosses at the time told me the decision was based on my inability to carry out my job, and that I wasn't a good fit for the company.

It was an easy out for the company to let me go without having to actually fire me for "being too Black and making us feel uncomfortable by challenging our blind spots relating to race." The moment that Black women are no longer viewed as palatable to white people, we are seen as a threat—aggressive, problematic, complainers—and dropped without any self-reflection or self-work on their part. It wasn't until international attention was paid to Black issues that my ex-boss and former teammates not only recognized our company's blind spots but also started to take action to combat their faults. This delayed action speaks volumes—white business leaders and employees are perfectly willing to disregard Black opinions until those opinions receive widespread attention and respect from other white people.

Trying to appeal to white people but receiving very little in return has caused me to drop code-switching almost entirely. I no longer worry about how my hair is styled before a job interview or make my Instagram account private so my non-Black coworkers won't make faulty assumptions about me and my friends. I'm not interested in presenting a watered-down, boring version of myself to be considered worthy of respect, a job opportunity, or a promotion. It's why so many of my Black woman friends working in various industries, and myself included, aspire to leave corporate life to work for ourselves—free from reporting to and working alongside people who meet us with biases and microaggressions.

We aren't necessarily welcome at these companies that vouch for being open-minded and inclusive. So long as we are catering to their habits, styles, and customs, we might then stand a chance at advancing, but the ladder of advancement only has so many rungs for Black women. The biased systems run by people who genuinely believe they are not biased are what push Black women out of these spaces. What white progressives—and even non-white progressives such as my younger self—do not fully understand is that the difference between themselves and Black women is not just the color of their skin. It is also our culture, our expression, our customs, and our language. It is not enough to accept us for the difference in the shade of our skin but not the differences in our entire being. What I mean is, many white liberals have successfully managed to not use someone's skin tone as a factor for whether they'll be welcoming to them but unconsciously still use someone's customs, expression, and style to alienate them. This sometimes forces Black women to tokenize themselves for survival, when really, we should be accepted entirely.

CHAPTER 5

Policing without a Badge

One summer in Los Angeles, while shopping on Melrose with my boyfriend, a white woman threatened to call the police on me after hitting our car. I had finished my shopping before my boyfriend and didn't feel like waiting around while he continued his shopping, so I headed back to the car early. Once I made it back to our car, another car pulled in to park in front of us. I sat in the driver's seat, scrolling through Instagram, when suddenly I felt the entire car shake. I honked instantly to alert the driver that they were hitting my car. Then I waited nearly five minutes for them to get out of their vehicle. After all, they had just parked, so I figured they'd be getting out soon. I also wasn't going to approach them, not knowing who was in the other car or what kind of emotions they might be feeling after the accident. Even the smallest fender benders tend to create hostile environments, and I wanted to avoid any kind of aggression. So instead, I took a photo with my phone, through the front window, of the license plate in front of me. That's when a rushed, young white woman finally stepped out of the vehicle. She hurried over to the parking meter to pay, without acknowledging me or my car, so I rolled down my window and confronted her. "Excuse me, you know you hit my car, right?" I called out to her. She looked at me with surprise and responded with something like "What are you talking about?" and continued to pay the parking meter. I was pissed. What could have been a simple settlement was going to turn into some unnecessary argument because this woman was not willing to take responsibility for her actions. Keeping my tone at a normal volume, I said, "You heard me honking multiple times, right? You felt your car hit something, right? Surely, you were aware of that." As people started passing by and observing the conversation, the woman denied the accident totally. We went back and forth on whether she hit the car or not, and she continued to say I was lying, prompting me to step outside the car and show her the damage itself. I quickly texted my boyfriend, "come to the car, someone hit it," and opened the door to step out. This is when the woman's demeanor changed entirely. She started to yell at me not to get out of my car and shouted that she felt threatened by me. She claimed I was overreacting and that she would call the police. I argued back with her, losing my patience but maintaining my temper. Then I took a picture of the obvious damage to the car, a dent about the size of a tennis ball and got back in the car. Right then, my boyfriend started to approach the car from across the street. He didn't speak to me or even acknowledge my presence, causing the woman to think he was just a curious bystander. Or possibly someone coming to help her. He started to take photos of the damage, and then the woman turned to him, crying, and with the softest voice ever said something along the lines of "I don't know why she's being so aggressive toward me, she keeps saying I hit her car." I was in shock at how quickly she went from someone yelling furiously at me to a soft-spoken victim with tears in her eyes. In any other situation, I would have felt powerless next to her tears and false story, but luckily the person she was seeking help from was someone who already had my back. Shock, embarrassment, and anger filled her face when my boyfriend responded, "That's our car that you hit. Do you have insurance?" Maybe she figured my boyfriend was a bystander and unrelated to me because he's a white man. Maybe she assumed he would take her side and believe her lies, viewing her as a victim, because she felt she held power over me as a white woman. Whatever delusion was behind her thinking, I knew it was a form of self-victimization, one that posed herself as teary-eyed and innocent and the other person as the aggressor. It was a form of policing and manipulation this woman had been conditioned to think would work in her favor and pull her out of situations where she was in the wrong.

Oftentimes when white women cry in situations involving other women—specifically Black women—Black women instantly lose any regard they might have had. And I believe the white women who choose to do this—exercise their privilege—know this. Either that, or their fragility gets the best of them so that the slightest inconveniences result in tantrums and tears. Or maybe they're so unaccustomed to being held accountable that in the few times they are, it's too much for them to deal with. Whatever the reason might be, white women who use tears to self-victimize, in situations where they are not the victim, need to leave this century-old habit behind. Not only is crying about the simplest of things a childish behavior; it causes non-white people to not believe white women when they actually are crying about something serious or reporting an important issue. Ultimately, it's a form of policing because white women's tears are powerful enough to control situations by shifting the blame off them and onto someone else.

In a viral TikTok, a video of a white woman flexing her ability to cry on cue, at any moment she wants, backfired. I assume the woman in the video thought the clip was a cute idea, a way to show off a skill, but the unanimous responses from other users called her out for this dangerous behavior. The comments section largely echoed the belief that some white women use fake tears as a tool to manipulate others and hold power in situations where they want control. One person commented that white women have been using their tears to manipulate people and situations for centuries dating back to Emmett Till, who might still be alive if not for a racist white woman claiming she felt threatened by him. Today society refers to racist white women who manipulate people with their fake tears and self-victimize in situations where they are the aggressor with a term, or more precisely, a name: *Karen*.

This is the kind of white woman who asks the little Black girl in her neighborhood for proof of certification for her lemonade stand, or calls the cops on a Black family barbecuing and playing loud music in a nearby public park. Karen is the modern-day irritated wife of a slaveholder; she embodies the same entitlement as Carolyn Bryant (the woman responsible for Emmett Till's murder); she resembles every white woman during Jim Crow who bound themselves to a racist man, completely forgoing their "mothering nature" to disable the Black community. Karenism stems from white women's victimhood, constructed by a plethora of myths during the era of American slavery. Despite slave masters raping their slaves, Black male slaves were the ones portrayed as sexual threats to the white wives and daughters of slave owners. This ideology created the accepted belief that white women needed to be protected by white men, no matter how simple the reason, directly justifying racial violence toward Black men and women. For decades, white women have been exercising their power, oftentimes with no repercussions, suggesting that Karenism isn't a new act, it just has an updated name.

Karen, while often associated with a conservative, unattractive, older white woman, does not actually discriminate by age, beauty, or political status. Karen could be a twenty-two-year-old, attractive white woman accusing a Black teen of stealing her phone in a hotel lobby; she could be a Democrat, Obama-supporting dog owner calling the cops on a

Black bird-watcher in Central Park; Karen could be in the workplace, preparing an unnecessary email to the boss of a coworker because instead of addressing any concern directly, she reports every little discomfort to someone in power, in an effort to punish people. Karen feels she is owed something. Karen wants to be served. And she doesn't care if obtaining these things puts other peoples' lives in jeopardy by involving law enforcement. This country has a history of white women falsely accusing Black people of doing things—from whistling to rape to attacking them at the mall—yet for some reason, even some progressive-identifying white women have normalized this behavior instead of working to dismantle it.

Personally, I hate the term *Karen*. No other subgroup has been afforded a harmless name to describe their harmful behavior other than white women. In my opinion, giving dangerous behavior a simple English name humanizes the person at fault—and it baffles me that even when white women are putting others in danger, we still find ways to joke about their actions. Karen is a meme, but the women who are labeled as such should be referred to as racist white women. Not Karens, not Pamelas, not Susans, but racist white women. The use of viral monikers becomes problematic when it assigns an innocuous and anonymous name to a person who has seemingly committed overtly racist actions. When white men commit overtly racist actions, we do not refer to them as Bob, or Mike, or Tom. We call them racist white men. Even my white female friends enjoy referring to racist white men as racists but racist white women as Karens. And during Halloween of 2021, costume stores began selling Karen costumes, further pushing the idea that white women can dress up as someone racist, which directly separates them from racist white women or their own racist behaviors and practices, whether conscious or not. In this distinction, liberal-identifying white women are able to separate themselves from white men, who, although they are also white, are more privileged because of their gender. In dehumanizing racist white men, but humanizing racist white women, self-proclaimed progressive white women have created a narrative that separates themselves from other white women simply by omitting the shared identity: white woman. For a while now, but mostly after the racial reckoning that occurred during summer 2020, some white liberals have started to digitally separate themselves from other whites who do not publicly align with their social views regarding race. But that separation often isn't as authentic as it appears. Many self-professed liberal whites still socialize with, befriend, and date less progressive whites, shift their focus on separating themselves from them rather than educating them, and develop this false belief that they do not carry out any forms of racism. This separation to the public, but not behind closed doors, enables harm against Black women in the form of policing because no one is actually putting an end to the behavior; they're just choosing to distance themselves from it. My friend Gabrielle Inhofe, a white woman herself, shared similar sentiments regarding the self-protection white liberals try to create for themselves by not identifying with their community on her Instagram Story:

Been thinking a lot lately about the classification of [all] white people, and I do think it's 100% fair to group us together, despite variations in how progressive we are. I think white liberals spend too much time trying to differentiate ourselves from blatant racists, that we fail to take accountability for our implicit and insidious—and often more everyday and harmful—brand of racism. By focusing on big instances of racism, and touting our own alleged wokeness, we fail to assess where we fall short—and often exhibit white fragility when we do encounter shortcomings. Additionally, no matter how progressive, every white person still benefits from systemic racism. We have all been socialized in a systemically racist milieu. Even if not actively racist, we often passively enable racism, especially as we all know and normalize relationships with white people who are much less progressive. So when we hear "all white people…" well, yes. I think that's an accurate grouping that we must accept.

When a heated white woman attacked a Black woman at Victoria's Secret in 2021 and self-victimized in the process, my white women friends shared the video on their social media accounts with comments like "fucking Karens" or "Karens are so crazy." It's easier than saying "fucking white women" or "white women are so crazy" when you, too, are a white woman and don't want to draw attention to the obvious fact that you two are of the same identity. So long as some white women continue to use innocuous and anonymous names for people who look very much like them, their mother, and their grandmother, in order to separate themselves, the problem will not be resolved. What most progressive and liberal white women should recognize is that Karen-like characteristics can be ingrained in them too. But in sharing videos that show the extreme version of Karen-like traits—victimizing oneself, putting a Black person in harm's way, refusal to be held accountable, calling the cops, throwing tantrums in public, invoking their struggle with mental health to avoid taking responsibility for their racism, crying white-woman tears—average white women feel they cannot relate to such harmful behavior. While many liberal white women may not actively intend to harm Black people like Karens do, they do less blatantly carry out these same practices in the office, at school, and even online.

When I was working at one of my past jobs in New York, I experienced a situation at work that highlighted the power of the white-victim narrative. What started as my simple request to send me updates about missed events on days that I'm out of office quickly turned into a three-month-long investigation with the HR department. At this job, I didn't work on Fridays, so I would often miss out on invites to events that were posted in our team's Slack channel. One Thursday, before breaking for lunch, I asked my coworker if she would mind texting me about any events posted on Friday that I might miss. It seemed like a simple ask for a coworker, let alone a friend, but her reaction to my request said otherwise. She told me over Slack that she was overwhelmed with work and in a bad mood, and that it wasn't her responsibility to keep tabs for me. And she was right, it wasn't her responsibility, and she could have respectfully declined. Instead, the conversation resulted in a series of messages where she was practically going off on me for asking her to do me a favor. One message even said something along the lines of "don't test me today." Typically, I would write this kind of behavior off, but I could see that she was beginning to get worked up, and she was prone to frequently cry at work, which, in almost all cases, elicited an empathetic response from our manager and coworkers. All of this led me to distrust the response from our manager, or the HR department, if this coworker were to escalate things herself. Often HR departments protect and side with their white employees while gaslighting or disregarding the concerns of Black employees. So I felt I needed to take the lead on pushing this situation forward in order to tell my side of the story first. I forwarded the messages to our boss, who was also close with the coworker in question, and asked him to address the issue with her, but he pushed back. I remember feeling furious and somewhat hopeless because I should not have even had to advocate for myself in this kind of situation. I voiced that her language would have resulted in an explosion had I sent a similar message to her, and that it was important for her to be made aware that it is simply unprofessional to talk to people in that way at work. My boss pushed back on the concerns I was raising in our messages and kept asking if I felt threatened by it. I told him no, but that it wasn't about whether I felt threatened or not, it was about her inappropriate language toward me and, even more, that this would not be acceptable had I been the one to send this message. The three of us were called into a conference room to discuss the messages my coworker had sent—and this is when things took a turn. When we met in the room, she was visibly upset about us meeting in the first place. My boss asked me to explain what happened, and I read the Slack messages from my phone, showcasing the escalation of a simple request to an inappropriate verbal exchange. I told my coworker that I didn't appreciate how she had spoken to me, and that's when my boss turned to her and told her that her language was unacceptable and asked her to apologize. And that would have put things to rest, but then she immediately burst into tears. Instead of simply apologizing for her outburst, which would have cleared the air and allowed us to go back to our desks, she sobbed and started yelling things like "I told you I was having a bad day" and "you were being aggressive toward me." I was floored, because never had I imagined myself being in this kind of situation. I just stared at her, part of me trying not to laugh at how stereotypical this response was, but the other part of me appalled by how ingrained this reaction could be for some women. My boss immediately started to comfort her and ask her if she was okay. I could see that I was losing my grip on the matter at hand, and that this was now becoming a larger issue, separate from the issue that brought us here. I wondered if she even knew what she was crying about, and quickly answered the question for myself: not only was this a way of eliciting a reaction from people and getting her way, I think she was also likely overwhelmed by being questioned about her behavior. White women don't get questioned very often, if at all, so I wasn't shocked that she was becoming upset over having her actions called inappropriate or for being asked to apologize, which would mean she was at fault for something. The crying continued to grow louder, with her going on about how she was feeling attacked, how she isn't a bad person, how she felt *I* was being aggressive. I stopped her again because I wasn't going to allow anyone to label me as aggressive when I didn't do anything to bring us into this room. I told her that as a Black woman, I did not want that stereotype placed on me. I told her that if anyone was being aggressive, it was her who was yelling and had previously warned me not to test her. My demeanor stayed calm as hers continued to grow with anger, until she stood up and yelled, "Fuck it, I quit." Then she ran out of the conference room crying. My boss looked shocked, as if he didn't know what to do next. I wasn't shocked by her actions at all. I will say, however, I *was* shocked to see her back in the office the very next day after having announced to us that she was quitting. I was even more surprised that her behavior in the conference room was being dismissed and that we were expected to carry on as usual. Had that been me, screaming and crying in the office, I'm sure I would have been asked to leave, or been escorted out. I would have been viewed as a threat, or at least as unprofessional. When consulting my

Black coworkers on how to best handle the situation, they agreed that her whiteness privileged her—whereas this kind of behavior would have likely cost me my job.

When white people in work environments are not held accountable for their actions, they continue to repeat the same actions, normalizing this behavior, and nothing changes. While I had no interest in "punishing" my coworker or hurting her job in any way, my Black colleagues and I had seen so many of our white colleagues go to HR for much smaller incidents than what had happened to me. My instinct is almost always to keep my head down and let things go, but in this case it felt like taking this to HR was the right thing to do, especially given how public the incident had been and how I knew it was likely to be interpreted by our colleagues, who had simply seen my coworker cry then storm out of the room we'd been in. When I explained all of this to my boss, he pleaded with me to reconsider and to understand that my coworker was just having a bad day. I told him that Black women don't get to have bad days like that in the office and that I would have been fired immediately had I behaved in the same way.

Taking the situation to HR resulted in a three-month-long investigation. The process was so drawn out, and I remember feeling like dropping the investigation altogether, but I figured they were drawing it out for exactly that reason. At one point, the HR professional asked me if I was willing to let it go because my coworker was sorry. I told her I would at least like to hear, from her, that she was sorry. I told them this type of behavior was not uncommon at this company and several of the Black employees had stark examples of unprofessional situations they'd been subjected to at the hands of white co-workers who were never held accountable. So they allowed us to meet together. My coworker apologized and cried during the entire meeting. I could see that the HR team felt really bad for her and felt agitated with me for putting her in a situation that elicited tears. She had become the victim in the situation—a victim of being held accountable, and that was enough to push the blame away from her and turn me into a "difficult" employee.

I want to end this story by saying that I personally do not believe that my ex-coworker acted maliciously or had any ill intent. I think, more than anything, that a lack of awareness found in so many privileged people played a role in how, at the time, my coworker didn't understand the negative effects her behavior could have on how I was perceived in the office, or the potential danger that it could pose to my employment. I don't think that her tears were calculated, but rather likely a reaction to being held accountable and of potentially feeling uncomfortable with not only being in the wrong but also having to admit to it. That display of emotion cast her in a position of "weakness" that garnered sympathy in a situation that could easily have cost me my job.

Tears are not the only form of overuse of power—moving blame onto someone else out of fear of repercussions or just outright entitlement—that I've experienced in the workplace. In fact, the most frequent form of policing Black women I know are subjected to on a daily basis is tone policing. By definition, tone policing is a conversational tactic that dismisses the ideas being communicated when they are perceived to be delivered in an angry, frustrated, sad, fearful, or otherwise emotionally charged manner. It's become a widely used strategy, both in personal situations and work environments, to derail conversations about tough and touchy topics, or a tactic used to shift blame from one person to another. Tone policing is most popularly used against marginalized people when the conversation focuses on race, or when someone is being confronted or held accountable for some mistake. The practice closely aligns with a reaction of white fragility and the unwillingness to accept one's role in a difficult situation. Like white tears, it is a frequently used manipulation tactic that some white people employ to camouflage their unreasonably authoritative behavior.

As a writer who often covers culture analysis and race, I sometimes receive messages from readers who claim they are open to learning more about the topic I'm reporting on but were turned off by the tone in my writing. And yes, in case you're wondering, these emails have come from only white people. One email specifically, in response to an article I wrote for *The Guardian* titled "White Clicktivism: Why Are Some Americans Woke Online but Not in Real Life?," was from a white woman criticizing my approach and deciding my tone was to blame for white people not wanting to change:

> Ms. Holt, I read your article in The Guardian today and
> as a white liberal woman in her mid 30s who takes pride

in educating my peers about their white privilege and votes in local elections, I do not think the message you are trying to convey will be well received by the majority of your readers. Am I not considered "woke" since I use my social media to share infographics but don't feel like letting go of all my less progressive friends and family members? What about all the work I do behind the scenes? People have the right to choose how they want to show their progressiveness and being so abrasive and upset about a few of us still having friends who have a lot more learning to do is not going to bring white and black people together. And as someone who enjoys writing myself, using an aggressive tone rarely keeps anyone reading beyond the first couple of sentences.

Disguised as constructive criticism, the email was simply an attempt to derail the analysis I gave by focusing on my tone. The reader was upset with the article bringing attention to one of her own blind spots regarding allyship, and instead of using the piece as a means to educate herself, she felt the need to attack me for doing just that—educating her, and other people. By stating that my tone was aggressive, she stereotyped me as the angry Black woman. And by introducing herself as liberal and giving examples of why she labels herself as such, she attempted to place herself in a position of knowledge, as if she as a self-identifying white woman is absolved of racism and can't learn anything about racism from a Black woman. Ultimately, she missed the point of the article, which never mentioned "letting go of all my less progressive friends and family members" but instead recommended cutting off ties with racist friends and family members who are not willing to change.

When I put out a tweet asking Black women to tell me about their encounters with tone policing, more than forty women reached out to me within an hour of posting. Stories varied. Some were tone policed by managers and clients. Some shared being tone policed by romantic partners, while others voiced being tone policed by friends. Some cases of tone policing were less obvious to people, like a manager telling them they seemed annoyed or frustrated when they really weren't. Other cases were more obvious, like being labeled as aggressive or combative in situations where the person tone policing was in the wrong. In almost all situations, the people policing these women's tones were white men and women, but mostly white women.

One thirty-one-year-old Black woman living in Los Angeles told me about a situation where she was tone policed by a friend when calling out the friend for doing something wrong. Her story mirrored my encounters with tone policing, both with the woman who hit my car and with my ex-coworker at my past media job.

> I had a friend—whom we are no longer friends—a white woman, who wants to be a TikTok influencer and in her pursuit of attention and clout, she leaned into an audio

clip that was trending at the time that used the N-word. She used this audio with herself as the focal point and this really bothered me because I felt like this is a person that I've talked extensively with about cultural appropriation and white people feeling entitled to words, phrases, behaviors, and community that is not theirs, and then not wanting to deal with the consequences of that when they get called out. So I had a conversation with her about it and was trying to get her to understand why this was hurtful to me and all she could focus on was that I wasn't speaking to her in a tone that she liked. There was no "I'm sorry for hurting you as my friend. I'm sorry for doing things that don't reflect what I say my values are." It was just, "I don't appreciate the tone with which you're speaking to me. I would never talk to you this way." Like it was all entirely focused on my tone and I feel like she did that to remove the blame from her in this situation, and instead make me out to be the person who did something wrong.

A similar situation occurred with a thirty-two-year-old Black woman living in Upper Marlboro, Maryland, who told me of one tone policing occasion involving her direct manager, a white woman, when she called her out for inappropriately touching her hair:

I have natural hair, so I often would wear my hair out or in twists. I came to work one day and I had my hair in twists and my manager was really intrigued by the style. She said she loved my hair and that she thought it was great. Then she reached over to touch my hair and my immediate reaction was to tell her please don't touch my hair. She was so caught off guard by me not wanting her touching my hair, and her response was something about wanting to see how long it actually is because she had heard something about shrinkage with curly hair. I told her we could talk about it, but I'd prefer if she didn't touch my hair. I even went further to explain why I don't like when people put their hands in my hair. We're in an office environment, I just came into work, I don't know what else you've been doing. Whether you've been eating breakfast or typing on your computer. I just prefer if you don't touch my hair. Then her vibe shifted from "I was curious" to "well, you're making it seem like I'm trying to harm you." And I explained that no, it's just my personal preference that people not touch my hair unless they're actually styling my hair as a stylist. It was a very awkward situation because we're at work and this conversation isn't even about work and she was being combative with me by just simply stating my boundaries. She kept asking me why I was being forceful and aggressive, and that my tone was making her feel that way. It was jarring because she was the person being forceful after I said, "no, please don't do this." She kept insisting on why she should be able to do this, and then it turned into, "well, I just don't think that was very kind of you," and then it was about how I hurt her feelings. She claimed that it made her feel like she was a person trying to do something wrong to me, and that as my manager, she only wants the best for me. I felt like it was strange that she was trying to turn this into being about work when this really was about physical safety. All at once it was gaslighting, victimization, and tone policing, when she could have simply agreed to not touch my hair.

Another Black woman, twenty-nine, living in San Francisco, California, described being tone policed by a white manager as a way to disguise jealousy of how well she was performing at the company:

> My manager was a white woman who was a vice president at our global consulting firm. I was leading a lot of our website, digital projects, and some global brand projects, and we would have to present to senior leadership, which included the president and CEO of the company. During these presentations, I would explore the company's roadmap, where we are in terms of achieving goals, and then present my recommendations. And so after one of the meetings, my manager came to me and asked me to change how I would present my recommendations, and told me that my tone came off as if I knew everything. But this was my role. It specifically was my job to present to these senior leaders who were very far removed from

the tactical and technical aspects of the work that I'm doing for all intents and purposes. I am the subject matter expert on the topic and I am serving as the lead project manager for the project. I am talking to our outside vendors every day. I'm managing the internal team. And the feedback basically was that I'm not giving a good impression because my tone is coming off as [if] I know what we should be doing as a company, and that that wasn't my place. When I shared this feedback with our CEO, who was a Black man, he was shocked to find that my manager held that opinion, and he even sided with me. Ultimately, I realized she just didn't want me to be seen as the expert, because she later required that I put together the presentation, share it with her, and then she would present it on behalf of our team.

One thirty-year-old woman living in Detroit, Michigan, told me of the ways in which even her body language was constantly policed at work.

When people ask me a question and I don't really know the answer, or I'm trying to figure out the answer, I tend to look up. I've felt like the only people at my job who have made a big deal about this are white employees. They take it as me rolling my eyes at them, when really I'm just thinking before I'm responding. I've even been approached, randomly, by a coworker to ask me if I was okay because I was sitting with my arms crossed. When I told her I was fine, and that's just how I felt comfortable sitting, she persisted in telling me that my body language is making her feel like I'm in a bad mood or mad about something. I'm like damn, can you just go focus on your own self? I feel like white people in work environments want to overanalyze every little thing to try to create this perfect environment in their head, when really they're just going around unnecessarily policing everyone and it's creating the worst of environments. Why am I being perceived as rude or disrespectful just because I'm not sitting up perfectly straight, or smiling 24/7, or having my arms crossed?

Even highly successful Black women who are in the public eye are often subjected to tone policing. The most popular example of this would be Serena Williams, who is often made to feel like her anger is extreme and unreasonable or that her tone and body language are aggressive and threatening. During the 2018 US Open final, Williams received a code penalty for alleged coaching, a penalty point for breaking her racquet, and an additional game penalty for calling the umpire a "thief." The whole ordeal resulted in a fine of seventeen thousand dollars. While coaching violations in tennis happen often, it's rare that they're considered to be the player's fault, as opposed to the coaches' fault, so it makes sense why Williams felt she needed to defend herself in this situation. It's also pretty common for tennis players to express some form of frustration after a missed point or loss, but that expression doesn't always result in a fine. The *New York Post* called the outburst the "mother of all meltdowns." In a *Sportscasting* article titled "Serena Williams and Other Tennis Players Who Had the Worst Meltdowns," reporter Jess Bolluyt ranks the six "worst meltdowns in tennis history" in order of least to greatest. Despite Williams's argument with umpire Carlos Ramos during her match against Naomi Osaka at the 2018 US Open being ranked as the least worst on the list, Williams is the only name mentioned in the article's title, the only player mentioned twice on the list, and the only person who had an outburst that involved calling out discrimination. The other four tennis players on the list are all white men, leaving out white female tennis players who have also had outbursts during matches, like CoCo Vandeweghe yelling, "Fuck off, you fucking bitch," at her opponent during the 2018 Australian Open just earlier that year.

Policing and the biased perception people have of Williams might explain why so much focus is given to Williams's outbursts and not so much those of other tennis players. It's widely known, from negative media portrayal to excessive drug testing and strict enforcement of rules during matches, that Williams has received the brunt of extreme policing throughout her career. She knows the underlying context of this treatment, making it more than reasonable to assume that Williams, like anyone else, would be angry, especially when comparing her situation to that of other tennis players. Her anger, however, at the 2018 US Open was met with a fine, as a way to silence her and remove power from her status. The excessive and unique code violation itself—which cost Williams a game—was a form of policing.

Outside of the governing body, the belief that white people need to police and hold authority over Black bodies is highly prevalent in white culture. The barbaric white man and his son who murdered Ahmaud Arbery while he was jogging in their neighborhood in February 2020 because they decided that exercising was "suspicious"; the aggressive white woman who called the cops on Christian Cooper while he was bird-watching in New York's Central Park in 2021; the white man who, in July of 2019, called the police on Wesly Michel while he was waiting for friend at an apartment building, are just a few mainstream examples of the never-ending inherent polic-ing of Blackness by white people. This policing is almost al-ways for trivial reasons, like ordinary or inconsequential activities, suggesting policing of Black people is still heavily ingrained in a culture that historically policed Blacks through enslavement, murder, rape, and discriminatory laws and practices. How much has changed when there are white women calling the cops so often on Black people that a name has been given to the character? How many steps forward have we taken when racially driven phony calls to the police have caused lawmakers to propose legislation to curb the practice? How far along are we as a society when the practice of policing Black people becomes such a frequent, uncon-scious behavior that it is almost expected?

Historically, Black women have been policed in America since our earliest settling, through rape, beatings, and murder. Whether it be how we wear our natural hair and the clothing we choose to cover our bodies with, or our tone of voice and how we carry ourselves, or extremes like involving authority or holding authority over us in situations that do not require such policing, young Black women today continue to be patrolled and controlled because a society founded on white supremacist ideology does not grant Black women freedom to be. Our society must distance itself from this ingrained and often unconscious need to control young Black women by unlearning authoritative culture and practices that have been passed on for decades. But more importantly, individuals must recognize when they might be carrying out this behavior and make an active decision to let young Black women exist and be themselves.

CHAPTER 6

Burnt the Hell Out

Two months into my first job in public relations—where I was responsible for managing numerous social media accounts for our clients—I was stressed beyond measure. Not only was I brought on as the only social media strategist for the entire company; I was the only non-white person within the organization. It didn't help me feel any more welcome that all of our clients were white too. Trying to convince my boss that we should utilize inclusive practices in our social media strategy was equivalent to beating a dead horse. I was constantly shrinking myself in order to be palatable, my judgment was consistently second-guessed, and my ideas were always turned down. To say I was overstretched would be an understatement. I was burnt out. Then a year later, when I started a new job as an editor at an online publication, I was expected to edit all the work of a team of nearly fifteen writers and short-form video producers. Most of them were turning around two to three pieces of content per day, and I was the only editor on the team.

I convinced myself that working ten-hour days was normal, because my boss expected me to finish all my work before signing off. I only left my laptop to pee and ate my lunch at my desk to avoid submissions piling up. My boss rewarded my drive, but never with a raise or promotion, just verbal congratulations. After days when I was sick or took off for vacation, I'd return to a ton of peer-reviewed pieces that needed my review because there wasn't another editor to step in while I was away. I was expected to play catch-up while simultaneously carrying out my other duties. After five months of working in this role, I told my therapist I was developing tightness in my fingers and intense back pain. Her response: "You're physically burnt out."

Over the last decade, burnout has become a growing topic among sociologists and health professionals as workplace demands increase for the millennial generation. Articles detailing the increase in burnout, mostly due to work-life imbalance, lack of social support, and dysfunctional workplace dynamics, have brought attention to the dangerous work-related stress brought on by working longer hours for less pay than previous generations. Burnout can have numerous effects on the body, including excessive stress, fatigue, insomnia, and depression. More serious effects include heart disease, high blood pressure, type 2 diabetes, and vulnerability to illnesses. While millennials are the target group in the mainstream discussion surrounding burnout, women are more likely to experience it than men, and not so surprisingly, Black women suffer from burnout the most.

A recent study found that Black women experience "accelerated biological aging" as a result of repeated or prolonged stress, like, for example, the kind brought on by trying to prove one's worth in a discriminatory workplace, not being able to advance in one's career, frequent exposure to micro-aggressions, a lack of opportunities, and the pressure to be constantly "on." Add on long work hours, feeling undervalued, being underpaid, being expected to continuously educate your non-Black colleagues, being gaslighted about your concerns, not having anyone in HR who represents you, endless Slack messages, and a culture that prioritizes always being available, and burnout becomes an almost unavoidable condition for Black women in professional settings. According to Kenya Crawford, a Philadelphia-based licensed mental health counselor and consultant on topics such as anti-racism and mental health, burnout is especially inevitable for Black women, because our whole life has been centered around this narrative of proving our value so that we can stay at a job a little bit longer:

> When we're talking about burnout, we have to acknowledge that burnout is the product of the intersections of capitalism, racism, sexism, and so many other forms of oppression, but really at the root of that being capitalism. Yes, this is becoming a topic that is explored frequently in workspaces, but there isn't that proactive approach to dismantling burnout in the workspace. And I think specifically for Black women, what happens for us, there is this experience of

imposter syndrome that is telling us that we are already not supposed to be in this space and that the ways that we are deemed valuable is by what we provide, what we give, what we share. So when we're walking around with those two narratives in our heads and our bodies and our psyches, it's really hard to say, "I'm going to choose no right now. I'm going to choose myself right now," which I think inevitably is going to lead to burnout, especially for Black women.

It should come as no surprise that every Black woman I am friends with, myself included, has felt pushed out of almost every corporate job they've held since graduating college. Some felt they were underpaid, while others saw no hope for a raise or promotion unless they moved to a different company. Many also have expressed feeling lonely because they were the only Black woman, or one of the few Black women, on their team, or in the company at large. Even more friends say they fall victim to burnout from overwork, daily microaggressions, and unreasonable, unspoken expectations to educate their colleagues about racism. Like my Black women friends, I, too, have experienced all these things and been pushed so far beyond my physical and emotional limits at work that I have quit jobs without having a backup, been diagnosed with anxiety due to work-related stress, and changed careers entirely to obtain career advancement and a wage that would allow me to save money while paying rent in New York

City. Crawford finds these experiences to be common for Black women in the workplace, which is why she centers her work on bringing attention to the physical damage that can sometimes result from working in predominantly white workspaces:

> The effects of microaggressions show up in several ways. Sometimes my clients will tell me they've been having a lot of stomach issues, or a lot of behavioral changes, or chronic stress symptoms, or psychological disruptions. And when I tell them it's an effect from the microaggressions they're telling me about at work, they didn't even realize it was connected. Your body is always there to tell you something. I make it a point to tell my clients that I'm watching you wither away in this workspace.

Experiencing microaggressions over an extended period of time can create intergenerational trauma that has the power to impact the genetic makeup of marginalized people. In this case, Black women's health is being negatively impacted by continuously navigating discriminatory and racist environments. Aside from high blood pressure and hypertension formed from high stress levels due to racism, Black women get less sleep than their counterparts, are more likely to be diagnosed with a mental illness and report excessive drug use. In 2018, the *Journal of Black Psychology* gave this social phenomenon a name: *racial battle fatigue,* "in which persons who experience chronic racial discrimination develop physiological, psychological, and emotional strain due to excessive amounts of energy expended on race-related stressors." Crawford believes a lot of Black women don't realize the magnitude of these stressors on their well-being: "The long-term impact of this is actually worsening the conditions of Black folk. And if I'm doing this on a daily basis, there's continuous research that proves, on a long-term basis, this impacts our physical, genetic makeup. Which then leads to generational trauma, which we've already kind of started to name and start that conversation."

Understanding the impacts of racism is vital to create solutions to alleviate these effects and produce support systems to provide tools for stress reduction and stress management. But microaggressions, or statements, actions, or incidents regarded as instances of indirect, subtle, or unintentional discrimination against members of a marginalized group such as a racial or ethnic minority, are not the only forms of aggression Crawford sees Black women suffering from in the workplace. Others include microinvalidations, microinsults, and microassaults. According to Crawford, microinvalidations are statements that diminish your experiences of racialized oppression. For example, if after disclosing to your manager that you experienced something racist or uncomfortable, they respond with comments such as "Well, are you sure that's what they meant? I think they were just trying to make a joke.

Everything isn't about race." Microinsults are statements, behaviors, or actions that highlight when a person of color is
operating outside their racialized stereotype—for example, if
someone said something like "I'm so surprised you went to an
Ivy League institution." Microassaults are clear and direct
forms of oppression that can be verbal, nonverbal, or avoidant. For example, a white person holding tight to their purse
or bag when they see a Black person walking toward them on
the street:

> I find that there's this idea with the term
> "microaggressions" that because it's micro, it's smaller,
> right? It's not as impactful as overt racism or even
> forms of covert racism. But while these may be subtle,
> while these may be quick comments that maybe were
> intended to be a compliment, maybe were intended to
> actually deepen your connection with this person, the
> long-term impacts of these experiences impact our
> physical health, our mental health, our emotional
> health, and at our core, they disrupt our safety. They
> disrupt our ability to acknowledge that, in this
> space, I'm safe in this connection. I'm safe in this
> workplace. I'm safe in this relationship. So if we're
> consistently receiving these microaggressions on a
> daily basis, the subconscious mind starts to internalize
> those experiences, and your psyche is going to start to
> believe that you're less than. I think the piece around
> understanding microaggressions that folks are always
> challenging themselves to acknowledge is that just

because it is micro doesn't mean that it's disrupting or limiting the impact of these experiences.

When I was working at a tech company and news broke to some of my coworkers that I had a book deal and wrote articles for *The New York Times*, the reaction from some of my teammates was shock and disbelief instead of admiration and kudos. When I was explaining my book in detail to a white woman in upper management, she met my synopsis with "So it's like a legit book? Do you actually have a publisher?" The inability to believe that I, a Black woman, had talent outside of my role at this tech company, and had achieved such success in my career, was a microaggression itself. It wasn't the first time white people reacted with shock rather than praise when finding out about my achievements, and it most certainly will not be the last. Crawford believes that while white people are becoming more aware of microaggressions, they continue to frequently project them in sly comments that are meant to be compliments:

> They're not saying phrases like "You're so pretty for a Black girl," as often. I think there's been enough articles around that. But it is still showing up in these sly comments that are still meant to be complimentary. The whole "You're so smart" or "You're so articulate." Whereas I can see that would be a genuine compliment if it was coming from a Black woman, but coming from a white woman, I'm like, "What did you think I'd be?"

It's like this disbelief, this shock. So when we look at the twelve themes of microaggressions, disbelief of intelligence is one of them, and it has this message behind it that Black, indigenous, and people of color aren't as intelligent as white people. So when we do show up and show out, as we continuously do, they're shocked. And the question is, "What's leading you to be shocked right now? What's leading you to actually believe that I wasn't going to show up in these spaces?" I think that's a really profound aspect of microaggressions that is not always given enough conversation or space.

My experience with this form of subtle but harmful microaggression has had a negative impact on my confidence and abilities in every job I've held. My self-worth has been torn down every time a boss has questioned my expertise or ability to do a job that I was hired for. My self-esteem has been tested every time a coworker in the same position as me, who didn't work nearly as hard, or have work experience comparable to mine, has been offered a higher salary or a promotion. My confidence as a writer has been burned every time my boss praised another writer's pitches and told me to work more on my own, simply because the topic I was covering wasn't of interest to their white agenda.

The conversation surrounding work-related stress in my Black woman friend group has always boiled down to the niche, unspoken issues we suffer from as Black women and not so much about the common stresses of long work hours or disliking your boss's attitude that our white peers vent about. It suggests that Black women are experiencing their own kind of burnout, one that is more complex, less talked about, and underreported, and therefore less understood and less widely known to anyone other than Black women.

Throughout my entire career in journalism, I've never reported to a Black editor, nor have I worked alongside another full-time Black reporter. When Erin Overbey, a former archive editor at *The New Yorker*, shared stats revealing the reputable publication's lack of diverse bylines and editors, Black women led the race for most underrepresented. According to her data, *The New Yorker* has never published a Critic-at-Large review by a Black woman writer in its ninety-six-year existence; fewer than 0.01 percent of print features and critics' pieces have ever been edited by a Black editor in the last fifteen years; and the print magazine has published only four book reviews by African American women in those ninety-six years. Yet, *The New Yorker* is viewed as reputable and prestigious, while remaining a mostly white publication. It begs the question—how reputable can an organization that lacks diversity even be? This phenomenon—where organizations and corporations actively bypass employing people of color—is an environmental microaggression. When a community, a society, or media portrays and features mostly white people, or when a workplace and leadership are predominantly white, it sends a message to everyone else that you're an outsider, that you don't belong there, and that you're not welcome. Most of the companies I've worked for have been in New York City—one of the most diverse cities in the world—and have mostly only employed white people. It immediately signals to me that there's something wrong going on in that space and calls attention to these other forms of microaggressions that may not be verbal, that may not be coming out of someone's mouth, but that are reflected in someone's actions.

The data released about *The New Yorker* isn't the first time a Twitter thread has exposed the lack of opportunity and fair pay for Black women in my industry. In June 2020, various authors took to Twitter to share their book deal advances, exposing the pay disparities in the publishing industry. We quickly learned that bestselling Black woman authors, like Roxane Gay, received much lower advances than relatively unknown white debut authors. For example, Gay received a $15,000 advance for *Bad Feminist*, and $150,000 for *The Year I Learned Everything*, while debut white authors like Chip Cheek and Mandy Len Catron earned $800,000 and $400,000 advances, respectively. A spreadsheet was later created for authors to reveal their advance offer, publisher, race and gender, and details about their book, in order to bring light to the pay discrepancies in the publishing world. When a similar discussion around salaries in the media industry circulated on Twitter, another spreadsheet, exposing how much various publications were paying their writers and editors based on race, supported the finding that Black women are severely underpaid and undervalued at these organizations. This same data, and my firsthand experience with being underpaid and undervalued, is what drove me to exit the journalism industry in 2020, during the midst of a global pandemic. Without any promise of a new job, I found it more important to prioritize my mental health and work as a freelancer, and ultimately begin searching for a job in a better-paying industry than continue working my benefitless contract media job that overworked me and wouldn't pay me for vacation time during a very traumatic summer for Black people. Not only did I witness most of my white colleagues receive promotions and healthcare benefits, I realized the trust the company offered them through full-time employment would never happen for me, because to them, I was replaceable, contractual, a trial—despite leading and editing the team of writers to whom they granted full-time employment. It's how many Black women in the workplace feel—replaceable and untrusted. How few Black employees there are on the teams we work on, in the companies we work for, and on the executive branches that lead us is a stark reminder that we are not top of mind in any avenue of hiring, and that when we are afforded an opportunity, it is a rarity itself, causing us to navigate the workplace more cautiously. When you already don't see many people who look like you being promoted, getting raises, or being hired at all, you're going to think twice about everything you say and everything you do when dealing with the majority, because you know you aren't really welcome there.

My experience of being overqualified yet not trusted to successfully do my job, not paid fairly for the work I'm doing, and not supported by my team was commonly shared among the Black millennial women I interviewed for this chapter. But for those who struggle with believing the differing experiences of others, data exhibiting the ways in which Black women specifically face the greatest obstacles and discrimination in the workplace justifies our stories. Black women in America make only 64 percent of what white, non-Hispanic men are paid, are the highest unemployed group among women, and are less likely to receive promotions. While gender parity affects all women, regardless of race, mainstream and historical advocacy for fair pay has not benefited all women equally. According to a 2016 study conducted by Pew Research Center, "white women narrowed the wage gap in median hourly earnings by 22 cents from 1980 (when they earned, on average, 60 cents for every dollar earned by a white man) to 2015 (when they earned 82 cents). By comparison, Black women only narrowed that gap by 9 cents, from earning 56 cents for every dollar earned by a white man in 1980 to 65 cents today." Not only do Black women make less money hourly and yearly in comparison to white women, they're more likely to be let go from jobs when the economy experiences downfalls. During the height of the COVID-19 pandemic, Black women experienced the steepest drop in employment and had the slowest job recovery well into December 2021. Being that Black women are less likely to be hired, and more likely to be let go, a continuous cycle of constant fear of losing your job and not being able to find another is one of the many reasons Black women feel they have to prove and overwork themselves in the office, and continue to work at companies that mistreat them. Dealing with this on a daily basis accelerates burnout for us. We can't make a single mistake or we risk losing all credibility. We can't risk being unemployed or it might be months before we land our next gig.

When filmmaker Nikyatu Jusu tweeted, "Rarely do I meet Black women who are mediocre or even average in the professional spaces I navigate. That whole 'we have to be x times better' to exist in these very average spaces is not hyperbole," many of the Black women that I follow on Twitter and Instagram shared the tweet. It's understood among Black women that mediocrity is not an option. When we're hired into predominantly non-Black spaces, we're essentially being offered the opportunity to prove ourselves rather than the experience non-Black women have of being offered an opportunity itself. Biases and stereotypes characterizing Black women as lazy and underqualified, and an unspoken expectation to work extra, have resulted in Black women facing unique challenges and unrealistic expectations that non-Black women and men do not experience in the workplace.

Dating back to slavery, Black women, whether they were mothers, whether they were young or old, were expected to work in the field and in the homes of their slave masters. Meanwhile, white women lived an essentially labor-free life and took care of minor tasks at home, yet were still elevated within the social hierarchy. Following slavery, white women were homemakers in the '50s, and in the '70s they gained more independence, but they didn't have to provide for their families in the same ways as Black women. Historically, in America, white women haven't been expected to work as hard, while Black women *always* have. And therefore, today, we are expected to work harder. Yet modern assumptions that Black women do not work hard, are resistant to hard work, must be monitored to perform well, and should be satisfied with any job rather than deserving of the best job, dilute the extra time and effort we put into our jobs.

What options are Black women left with when dealing with a niche form of burnout that their white coworkers, white boss, and predominantly white HR department cannot even fathom? The best option would be for Black women to quit. And Crawford agrees. But only if that's the last resort. She first suggests that her Black woman clients try creating boundaries with their coworkers to avoid being subjected to stressful encounters filled with microaggressions and subtle racism. For Black women, that might look like not attending the company social or the team happy hour, or removing themselves from conversations that involve racial gaslighting. In situations that are less avoidable, like conversations with a manager, a direct report, or a colleague you're working on a project with, Crawford recommends creating boundaries in the conversations. Whether it be developing a general spiel or bringing conversations to an end before they become too deep, it's important for Black women to recognize when they are in a space that is not built around their comfort. But when these practices, and other outlets like rage work—screaming into a pillow or taking a kickboxing class—are no longer making a toxic environment manageable, Crawford believes Black women should develop an exit strategy, because no Black woman should be in a constant state of struggle. Whether it be setting up informational interviews or exploring additional jobs or different spaces, Black women should not be expected to stay in spaces where the trauma that we're already trying to dismantle and unpack is being continued.

However, it's not always simple to leave. In corporate America, it's frowned upon to hop from job to job. Essentially, the silent rule is to spend at least one year at a company before moving to the next, but in many cases, Black women are left with no choice but to exit, even if it's a role they love, because of a toxic work environment. Mary Balingit, a director of diversity, equity, and inclusion for a youth writing organization, claims most Black women ultimately get pushed out of a company and do not necessarily hop from one job to the next like their non-Black coworkers:

> I've seen some Black women stay at companies despite being treated really badly. And again, even despite the burnout, there's this fear of not having another opportunity. Or being there for so long, like the old school way of thinking where generally Black women, especially those from immigrant upbringings, are not taught to leave work. But now there's this new concept for us, young millennials, to be able to leave every two years. . . . Most of these younger Black women leave specifically because of burnout or always being asked

to do more, for less. And I've even seen this verbiage predominantly in white spaces and leadership that will try to make Black women feel like they should be grateful to have a job. Whether or not that's an entry-level job or a job in management, folks with that kind of power and privilege will be quick to tell people they should be grateful they even have a job in this economy, or they'll try to allude to stupid things like that.

One of my interviewees for this book, Amber, a twenty-nine-year-old commerce editor in New York, left her media job of three years after finding out she was the lowest-paid writer on her team and realizing that she had never received a promotion either, only merit raises. She felt she had exhausted all of her options in making her working conditions better. After finding out her white colleague with the same work experience was offered $10,000 more than her, and held a more senior title, she realized she was undervalued the moment her job offer came with a nonnegotiable requisite that did not exist in the conversation leading to her coworker's employment. Amber almost never had the opportunity to meet the page-view goals her boss assigned to her, not because she was a lazy worker or not good at her craft, but because her content focused heavily on Black identity and the company's readership was predominantly white. It didn't help that her articles were rarely boosted by the social media team in comparison to the work of others on her team, resulting in fewer views on her pieces and not meeting her metrics.

The discriminatory behavior and actions from leadership came once Amber joined an ERG, or employee resource group, as an outlet for support from others like her, and to be rewarded for more meaningful work. "When I joined an employee resource group, that was when I knew I wasn't going to ever be promoted. My boss and people on my team were so uncomfortable with the fact that I joined a group for Black solidarity and branched out in the company outside of my team," she told me, noting that acknowledging her Blackness created friction between her and her predominantly white team. "I think it comes down to the implicit biases that management had, that they did not want to deal with, and thus that affected me negatively."

When she gained the courage to address her concerns with her boss, she was met with only gaslighting. And when she approached HR with her concerns about her boss's response, she was gaslighted and told to talk to her boss again. So, without verbally advising it, through lack of support and offering no solution to her concerns, the company theoretically suggested that she find a new job, and so she did. But it wasn't the lack of support that bothered her as much as the company's and her colleagues' questionable collective verbal support for diversity and their self-identified progressive persona. "It's so hypocritical because these are the same people who say that they're all about diversity, and want everybody to succeed, and support feminism, and are all like 'let's do something about it' and then in practice they actually don't," she told me.

Essentially, the white people on her team were racially gaslighting her concerns, which Balingit finds to be the leading subtle issue Black women face in the workplace:

> I think gaslighting is the number one issue Black women are facing at work, and it's not as often talked about as microaggressions. There's the stereotype, the trope of being the angry Black woman at work, and so a lot of Black women tend to carry that into those spaces and they either go two ways. They're either afraid to speak up about anything that's happening, whether it's if they're experiencing microaggressions, or a crappy boss, or a crappy day. Just anything that happens to normal, regular people all the time—Black women have to suppress their emotions because they don't want to fall into that stereotype. Which is so mismanaged by a lot of people in the world when they don't know how to understand that's just a stereotype that's placed unfairly on Black women. And then when Black women do speak up, they're labeled as aggressive, angry, and bossy. And if you were to apply those same behaviors to non-Black women, it's labeled as assertive or powerful leadership. Black women, in particular, are gaslighted to make them feel like they're crossing a line.

During our chat, Balingit spoke passionately about her workplace observations and the impact unconscious biases have on turning what should be a welcoming work environment into a dreadful space for some. She feels being gaslighted is the most common subtle issue among Black women in the workplace; the angry Black woman is the most recurring stereotype, and also the reason why Amber avoided bringing up her concerns to her boss and HR after the first time didn't work in her favor:

> In my opinion, perpetuating the angry Black woman stereotype really damages the way a Black woman can show up at work. And can even block the path of how they can ascend to leadership because they're labeled as aggressive or bossy. I also see a lot of just being unheard when it comes to grievances. If Black women come to the workplace in a sad mood or if they've had a bad day, or maybe they're a little bit more quiet and not as socially interactive, you're automatically labeled as having an attitude, or they assume you're just not feeling the job, or you're lazy, or you're unfriendly. It's always a negative label and assumption. It's never "how are you doing?" or "hey, I noticed you're not feeling well today." It's always something like, "oh my God, she's so unfriendly" or, "oh my God, they're difficult to work with." I don't think anybody ever pauses and asks a Black woman what they've gone through, throughout the day, which is very ridiculous.

Meanwhile, throughout all of this, these same coworkers often claim to be progressive, woke advocates for diversity and fosterers of inclusivity. Like Balingit, Crawford sees racial gaslighting as common workplace practice among white people who are in denial of the ways in which they perpetuate racism themselves:

> Racial gaslighting is when someone aims to undermine your sanity or deny your reality, particularly around a racialized moment. Say you experienced a microaggression in the workplace, you go to HR and tell them about a microaggression and that you want to move forward with taking some sort of action. And then the person responds with, "Are you sure it's about race? Maybe you misinterpreted them, right? Maybe you don't really know what a microaggression is, or maybe they were just joking or there was no ill intent behind what they did." What I've really seen recently, especially with some companies now issuing "woke" statements about how they're changing their company and taking a stance against racism, is a lot of people in HR and in D&I positions will gaslight by saying they're committed to change and this person isn't microaggressing you, or this person went to the microaggression workshop so they can't be perpetrating a microaggression because they know what it is.

Others refer to this behavior as virtue signaling, or publicly expressing opinions or sentiments intended to demonstrate one's good character or the moral correctness of one's position on a particular issue. In her work, Balingit has found this practice to be almost second nature to some white people in the workplace, who do more talking than doing when it comes to making environments more fair and inclusive for everyone but themselves. She suggests that white people need to stop talking about what theoretically *could* change and what *could* happen, and instead spend that time actually making the change happen. The fabric of white supremacy and white supremacy culture and how that and white culture in general show up in the workplace are widely understood. Most people, white people included, are aware that it's going to take a while for people to do a real culture shift, and most people in corporate spaces have had a baseline level of education to know what diversity and inclusion looks like in the workplace. Research shows that beginning with changes within each division of a company will ultimately lead to a shift through the entire space overtime. Leaders can start with asking themselves a series of questions about their divisions, but they must be willing to give honest answers. Are we using outdated practices? Is the language outdated? Are we really, truly being inclusive? Most importantly, to actually change things within a company, people in leadership positions have to be okay with relinquishing some of their power and privilege in order to really level out what the workplace will look like culturally, as it relates to diversity and inclusion. This means shared power in making decisions. In her research, Balingit finds that, in terms of creating an inclusive and welcoming environment, a lot of Black women are doing powerful, transformative work at their companies but aren't receiving recognition for it because it's expected of them:

> More often than not, what a lot of people of color do, and are expected to do, is manage up because their managers are usually white and don't have the same lived experiences as they do. So they fall into the category of having to teach people what it means to be more inclusive, what it means to be more diverse, and that's incredibly exhausting and that goes hand in hand with burnout. You get tired of teaching somebody that. You get tired of advocating over and over again and trying to explain to white people why you belong in this space, or why we need more diversity, or why we need this event that's going to be inclusive, or why we need this recruitment strategy. So then you get burned out until you build a team that's solid enough to be able to call out leadership at the higher level.

It's a commonly shared experience that Black women, who are hired because a company claims to celebrate diverse perspectives, are then ostracized for being unapologetically Black. Many Black women also report being ostracized for their wins and achievements in the workplace by non-Black coworkers who display bitterness and discomfort with their success. When Amber became the vice president of her ERG and started hosting popular events that employees at her company gravitated toward, even more tension was formed between her and her team. Instead of celebrating her success and suggesting she host events that would benefit her team, her boss and teammates shunned her:

> Once I had that potential to be front-facing, they started to actively block me from any other opportunities. I was actively discouraged by my manager and team leads to pursue on-camera and front-facing content opportunities for the video team as "talent." Yet, the company, at large, encouraged employees to sign up for video appearances in order to strengthen their individual on-camera presence and get involved outside of their team. So when a video opportunity that I would probably be interested in came up, my team leads would schedule one-on-ones during popular filming and casting blocks to keep me from signing up. Sometimes they'd even assign me additional work if a producer asked me directly to be in a video. My team lead also—once I joined our company's African American ERG—did not recommend that I get promoted, despite being at the company for two years, because they figured my plate was already "full" with the work I was doing as VP of said African American ERG.

Professionalism, or the conduct, behavior, and attitude of someone in a work or business environment, varies by culture, but in most American corporate workplaces, professional standards are determined by leadership, which is often white. In many cases, professionalism acts as a social control mechanism that is employed to punish Black women who oppose conforming to societal norms that encourage them to be passive, servile, nonthreatening, and unseen. From natural hairstyles being deemed unprofessional to email etiquette as an avenue to tone police, white professionalism was built for white workspaces, long before Black people were considered to work alongside them as equals. Yet, these customs are still prevalent in today's workplace. When working at a large media company and witnessing white women cry in the office every week over the most minute interruptions, I became aware of the different standards professionalism held depending on one's race. Had I cried at work, it is likely I would have been deemed unprofessional and told that the workplace was not the proper environment for such behavior. But when my white women coworkers felt stressed from not completing their deadlines or being tasked with "too much work," everyone seemed to flock to them to offer support and lessen their stress. It becomes confusing, as a Black woman, to know what is acceptable and unacceptable at work when things like crying fits and outbursts are normalized for some people but can be perceived negatively for others. It explains why several Black women like Amber seek safe spaces in employee resource groups, create close circles in the workplace, work from secluded parts of the office, and even join social clubs outside of their job. Whether in the form of coworking offices or restaurant tables where members might gather for a meal, these spaces are meant to serve as a social connection, a career accelerant, and a respite for those who suffer more often from microaggressions, lower salaries, fewer leadership opportunities, sexual harassment, and negative stereotypes than their white counterparts in the workplace, which can eventually lead to burnout. The benefits are endless when people of color are provided with spaces where they can gather and where they can access and invest in companies that cater to them without having to go out of their way to locate them. Members might start businesses together, hire one another for jobs, and directly circulate the POC dollar—all feats that might be impossible for Black women navigating domineering, predominantly white workplaces.

Ultimately, that's the reason behind Ethel's Club, a Brooklyn-based social club for people of color. Founded in 2019, by Naj Austin, with the goal to create an inclusive environment where people of color could work and socialize without suffering from microaggressions or judgment, Ethel's originally existed as a physical coworking space but now exists as a digital environment because of the global pandemic. Previously a communal spot for people of color, where they could advise and consult with others, network, and vent about work situations, today the club's offerings and resources mimic those of what white people gain access to in predominantly white institutions and companies—like mentorship, advice, and familiarity. At Ethel's, members have access to POC-led classes and groups focused on traumatic healing, career advancement, money management, and more—a need in communities that are so often underrepresented. On the phone, Naj told me how the idea developed from a daily lived experience of being a Black woman in New York and just wanting to see things from a Black perspective and experience.

> When I go to an art gallery, I'm looking for Black artists. When I go to a film showing I'm looking for Black filmmakers, so I'm constantly seeking it. And it was really, really difficult to find—not impossible. I always want to make that really clear. Ethel's Club was not the first to ever center people of color or Black folks, but I think it was sort of disparate and spread out. You kind of had to be in the film world to know where to find Black filmmakers, you had to sort of be in the art world to know where to find Black artists, or who the up-and-coming Black photographers were. And I thought that it should be much simpler than that. It should be easy. I should be able to live a fully Black experience in every way, in terms of the products I use and what I watch, read, and listen to, and Ethel's Club was very much a testing ground for that want.

Because most Black people work in predominantly white spaces, offices, and companies, the search for like-minded people can be more difficult than it is for white colleagues. That's the magic of spaces like Ethel's Club—in a physical space, Black people and other people of color can engage with one another and see what magic happens. Naj has witnessed members of Ethel's Club go into business together; one such business, Black Film Archive, is an online living register of Black films.

The greatest misconception about social clubs tailored to a specific race, Naj tells me, is that they're segregating. But in most cases, the workplace itself is already a segregated space for Black women. Whether it be that we are the only Black woman on our team or are being subjected to microaggressions only made possible in a predominantly white environment, Black women experience a form of segregation simply by going to work. To those who voice that spaces like Ethel's Club are bad for diversity and push races apart, Naj doesn't entertain a response:

> I think I see the power and beauty of identity and all the multifaceted ways in which a person can exist. And I want to support and empower that, and to do that, you must see them as who they are and not pretend that everyone is the same and we live in a rainbow utopia. Those thoughts go in one ear—if they even get that far—and out the other. To pretend most spaces are not already segregated is silly, and also a very white practice that is rooted in pretending that the world is egalitarian and equal. When we started Ethel's Clubs, we had a couple of moments—always on Facebook—of people saying this is reverse racism and this is

whatever. And I truly, and I mean this in like the most wholehearted way, it didn't even create a pause in my day because I make a point to start conversations with people who understand how the world works. And if you believe that a space for people of color is discrimination against white people, then you don't understand how the world works. And I don't want to have a conversation with you because we're starting at two very different factual points. Like where does one even start in that conversation? And I'm not really willing to give history classes on the side.

Truthfully, it's quite common for Black women to feel pressured and expected to give history lessons to, and educate, their white colleagues in the workplace. Whether it be as a means to disrupt gaslighting and microaggressions or offer advice to better the company's office culture, being that Black women are often the most underrepresented group, there is a firsthand understanding of how to make unfair situations and spaces more equitable. Even in the interview process, Black women are praised for their understanding of diversity practices and the ways in which they plan to make the workplace more inclusive if they're hired. And sometimes, those ideas are stolen when Black women are not hired for a job. Other times, they're popularized by non-Black employees who were enlightened by the Black women they work with. One Black woman, age thirty-one, living in Boston, Massachusetts, has witnessed the ways in which her ideas were popularized by a white person at her company, leaving no credit or appropriate merit for her:

> At my last job, I suggested to my team, before we presented to management, that we include images of full Black women in our pitch deck, opposed to only using mixed women to represent our Black woman models. My team—which was all white, and one Asian woman—seemed dumbfounded on why that change needed to happen and hadn't even realized that the only images they chose for Black women were mixed women. So I had to explain to them that it's colorist to only choose the lightest, closest to Eurocentric version of a Black woman for all our pitches involving Black women. And then when it came time to present, this white woman on my team literally told management about the change we made, and then went on to explain why, as if it were her idea. And of course, my boss praised her for her inclusive eye, and probably even used this as a reason for promoting her later on. Mind you, she was the same white woman who needed an education lesson from me on why we needed to change out the images.

Balingit sees examples like this often in her work. In her last six years of working on diversity and inclusion practices for predominantly white companies, non-Black people stealing the ideas of Black women, and no one else stepping in to make things right, strongly holds Black women back from advancing in the workplace:

> The biggest thing of all is that I believe that Black women are incredibly underappreciated in the workplace, and definitely not acknowledged enough for their work. I think there's a lot of ideas that stem from Black women, culturally, in and outside of the workplace, that they don't get enough praise for or credit for. That could make you exit a company, a place, a role, almost immediately, because it's literally your ideas being brought to life by somebody completely different than you. I've seen that quite often. And so beyond the burnout of being asked to do more for less, there's also this kind of identity labor that comes with being a Black woman in the workplace. You're never compensated for that identity labor. You can be tokenized for it, they'll use you for all these marketing things, and claim they're incredibly diverse, but it's all surface-level lip service until it's ready to champion your actual ideas and promote you in a healthy way.

For Black women, the modern-day office can quickly transition from a place for building rapport and socializing with colleagues to a highly stressful environment. Maybe that's why so many Black women I interviewed shared a collective relief when the pandemic forced companies to go remote.

One Black woman, age thirty-one, living in Los Angeles,

expressed feeling a weight lifted from her shoulders when she was told she wouldn't have to go into an office everyday where she actively had to bite her tongue and be subjected to subtle racism. But even in digital settings, Black women continue to face unreasonable biases. Another Black woman, twenty-nine, living in New York City, worked as a lawyer at an online real estate company and expressed feeling hyperanalyzed since her boss and team could not actually see her working, in person.

> I always feel like I need to have my Slack status on "active" or else my boss might assume that I'm sitting at home, watching TV, or something. Or I have to constantly use exclamation points and smiling emojis in my messages to my boss so she won't think I have an attitude in my tone. I'm having way more check-ins than I did when we worked in the office, and I'm always having to make myself available for a meeting at any given time or else my boss will probably think I'm out running errands, when normally we would take outdoor breaks and time off for lunch when we're all in the office.

The constant monitoring and check-ins about our performance is another form of policing; this expectation to overwork ourselves in order to hold a job, be paid fairly, or receive a promotion ultimately results in burnout, and the belief that Black women should be grateful or glad they are given a job is a microaggression, altogether creating a toxic work environment for the Black woman employee. It seems that every obstacle Black women are up against in the workplace ties back to us being undervalued. We're paid less because we are not viewed as valuable components to a company, regardless of how important, even vital, our role is. We're let go more often than our non-Black peers because we are undervalued. The belief that we are lazy, not working hard enough, or slacking off stems from the belief that we are not nearly as valuable workers, women, or people.

Changing these conditions in the workplace is not impossible, but I have often heard leaders I've worked alongside suggest that making changes in a company feels "impossible" and that diversity and inclusion should be approached as a "marathon not a sprint." Ultimately, it comes down to friendly and decent white people getting uncomfortable, being inconvenienced, and challenging the status quo, which many are not ready to take on. As a result, the status quo often remains entrenched for decades, and instead of actual changes happening, discussions and meetings about how to fix diversity and inclusion issues are held over and over again, because being in verbal support of diversity is so self-satisfying that it negates the need to do anything more. Balingit believes the solution is for more Black women to lead in these roles:

> In the past I would have said find the allies in your workplace, which are your white bosses that actually care and have that power and privilege to be able to make the decisions. There are some well-meaning managers out there that might help you make the

decision. But the truth of the matter is in order for Black women and Black people to succeed in this corporate world, we need Black women with their hands on the levers that can create the change. So companies need to hire Black women en masse, in leadership roles. There needs to be a huge culture shift and change in the way that we hire and create access to the spaces that are so incredibly inaccessible for Black women, particularly. We should be rewriting what these systems look like. Do we really need to do seven different interviews and require three cover letters and a degree from this specific university? It's just so incredibly inaccessible, and in that process alone, you get a lot of folks that fall out. They're just like, "It's way too much. I'm not even gonna apply for it." So we have to make it a little bit more accessible.

Balingit is right in that several job requirements make roles inaccessible to Black women who do not often have the time or financial resources to wait through a six-interview, two-month-long hiring process while unemployed. Or for Black women who have attended HBCUs, colleges that have historically been overlooked by companies seeking recent grads. As for myself, I've never feared not being able to obtain a job because I was underqualified or didn't interview well. I know for the most part, the only thing standing between me and landing a job that I interview for is oftentimes unconscious bias. While we're all taught to be ourselves when

interviewing for a new position, entry into a school, or place-
ment in a program, Black women have to be everything but.
In convincing a white person that we are worthy of the role
we are interested in, and going to perform well, we also have
to convince them that our Blackness is not going to result in
a negative outcome for them. If anyone should be able to understand this impossible standard, it should be white women,
who consistently lose leadership positions to white men. It's
assumed that a woman cannot lead a company or team as
effectively as a man because of stereotypes like being too emotional or less focused. And when women are pregnant or have
children, it's assumed they won't be nearly as dedicated to
their job as a man with children. These unsupported assumptions result in women making less money than men and receiving fewer business opportunities than men. Meanwhile,
Black women going up against white and non-Black women,
and men, also fall victim to unsupported assumptions. What
some white people in hiring positions fail to realize is the immediate shift in their own behavior once a new Black employee goes from candidate to full-time. It's as if the excitement
they once held for diversifying the team and bringing in a new
perspective crumbles once the new perspective is actually offered. There is great hypocrisy in continuously questioning
one's abilities, despite offering them a position after putting
them through several interviews and tests. It makes me wonder why we are hired in the first place. I believe this hypocrisy
boils down to unconscious biases that are *consciously* buried

during the hiring process, but *unconsciously* return once hiring is over. With diversity and inclusion being a leading topic in corporate America and on social media, recruiters, hiring managers, and employees of all levels are constantly being reminded to assess potential candidates and new employees without biases, to increase diversity hiring at the company. But race is only top of mind for them when *interviewing* a person of color. Bringing us in meets a quota, checks a box, and substitutes as a method of "doing the work." What isn't discussed nearly as often is the need to *remain* unbiased throughout a Black person's term of employment, and to be receptive to the diverse perspective and expression the company once claimed to be so welcoming of. Too many recruiters, hiring managers, and people in leadership roles fool themselves into thinking the work is done immediately after hiring a Black person into the company, and that simply by giving a Black person an opportunity, the company and its leadership are absolved from racism and unconscious biases. This same behavior plays out on teams as well, with lower-level employees who claim to want diverse team members and be in support of inclusivity but aren't welcoming to that new diverse hire when they become fully incorporated. I do believe that most white people who claim to be in support of inclusivity truly mean it, but how supportive can a person who has spent the majority of their life in spaces and social circles with people who look like them be? Are they likely to be experts in creating an inclusive environment if they spend the majority of their time in spaces that accommodate whiteness? In order to counteract a bubbled experience, educating oneself and making active choices about being in spaces that aren't centered around whiteness must be embedded into one's lifestyle.

When Issa Rae revealed in an interview with *Mic* that she initially included white characters in *Awkward Black Girl* and *Insecure* because a colleague advised her that it would help make "white people care" about her shows, it made me more aware of the tight grip white people hold on my career, and therefore my success.

During the summer of 2020, white people collectively took a newfound interest in Juneteenth. Being from Texas, I've celebrated Juneteenth my entire life. Every summer, my father would organize the Juneteenth parade in my hometown and I'd throw candy to the crowd from a float with my friends. It wasn't until I moved to New York that I realized Juneteenth was not a popularly known or celebrated holiday. It was a southern staple specifically because it marks the day when federal troops arrived in Galveston, Texas, to take control of the state and ensure that all enslaved people were freed. This didn't happen until 1865—two and a half years after the signing of the Emancipation Proclamation. In June 2021, Juneteenth became a federal holiday, after increased interest from the summer before. It was also the summer before when I was approached by *The New York Times* and commissioned to write an opinion piece about celebrating Juneteenth in Texas. Ultimately, that viral piece, on a topic I pitched to other publications several times prior to that summer, is what led to me signing with a literary agency, and then landing a book deal. While I've been elated by the aftermath of penning this viral article, it bothers me that it wasn't until white people collectively decided to recognize the holiday that I was granted the opportunity to write about it. It bothered me even more that my success that summer came at the expense of uncovering racial trauma inflicted by the white community on my community, in order to educate and enlighten the white community.

During the "summer of listening and learning," I wrote more articles than I ever had in my entire career as a freelancer. I was tapped every week by numerous publications to cover Black history, Black identity, Black culture, Black pain, Black death, and so on. Most of these publications were organizations I had applied to for full-time employment or pitched to in the past. But my applications were always denied and my pitches that focused on race turned down, until a temporary massive interest in racism erupted among white people, and there was finally a need for someone like me to tell stories that often were overlooked in a predominantly white newsroom. So I, and several other talented Black writers, were probed, for the benefit of educating white people. I feared I would burn out from the mental exhaustion of working a full-time job, meeting daily deadlines for articles, and covering topics that were traumatic and hit close to home, all during quarantine, a petrifying presidential election, and an ongoing surge of police brutality against my community. But I overworked myself anyway, or played the game, because I knew it could be years before I was ever given these "opportunities" again. Like Issa Rae, I am now at a successful place, where I do not have to entertain centering white people in my work in order to have my work considered, as they have never really centered Black people in theirs, but the journey leading up to here was draining.

In a piece exploring the unwritten rules of Black TV, *Atlantic* reporter Hannah Giorgis brings attention to the ways in which Black TV writers are not permitted to cover the Black experience authentically, when led by white showrunners and executives. Instead, Black TV writers are tasked with producing "negotiated authenticity... Blackness, sure, but only of a kind that is acceptable to white showrunners, studio executives, and viewers." White people in TV and film, despite an increase in Black representation when compared to decades before, still determine what the Black experience is and then hire Black writers to assemble it in a way that is digestible for a white audience. As Giorgis stated, "For decades, Black writers were shut out of the rooms in which those notions were scripted, and even today, they must navigate a set of implicit rules established by white executives—all while fighting for the power to write rules of their own." It reminds me of the Black experience across all industries, not just TV and film, or journalism, but healthcare, academia, sports, and so on. The implicit biases that white people hold in all areas of work result in Black women watering down their identity when picked for their diverse perspective, being silenced when asked to speak, and pushed out when offered to join. Until white people truly take a step back and allow others who have more experience with, and are more educated in working and interacting with, people from different identities to take the lead, the workplace will remain a toxic place for Black women, full of microaggressions, microinsults, microassaults, and burnout. We are rarely offered a seat at the table, and in the few instances when we are welcomed, we are not often allowed to bring our full selves or our full ideas. We're probed for our opinion and good judgment but frequently shut down and rejected as soon as that opinion or judgment offends the same "open-minded" person who probed us to begin with. For myself, working with white people, white women specifically, and more distinctively, self-identifying progressive, all-here-for-diversity white people, has proved to be an unpredictable feat. While clinging to their gender as a criterion for being marginalized but simultaneously exuding their whiteness as a means to hold power over my voice, some white women in the workplace claim to want representation for others but almost instantly create this imbalanced relationship filled with paralyzing biases.

Sooner or later, white people have to become more conscious of the ways in which they move, and need to be more honest with themselves, in order to see these problems can be fixed with their own efforts. In offering solutions and trying to locate ways to dismantle racism, we fail to realize that intellectualizing forms of oppression, particularly racism, is not going to be the thing that stops racism. You can throw books at it and you can throw articles at it. You can throw a plethora of information behind it, but if people are not checking their own relationship with white supremacy, it's never going to dismantle the issue. But if people are willing to do the work, to take action on a regular basis, only then will the workplace change to better accommodate Black women and allow us to be our full selves so that we won't have to sacrifice our careers because of burnout, exhaustion, or lack of community or upward mobility in the workplace.

CHAPTER 7

I Met God, She's Black

It's crazy to think that there was actually a time when I took pride in being called "strong." For me, it felt like one of the many attributes that made me an attractive human being. *Strong, pretty, hot, smart, intelligent, mature*—they were all words, in my opinion compliments, that I was used to hearing from friends, suitors, professors, my parents. Never did I imagine strength to be something that I would reject as it became less of a compliment and more of an expectation—something I was supposed to exude during times of weakness and turmoil.

This expectation of strength even showed up in my relationships. When I was twenty-four, I began dating Ian, a successful film director whom I had met through a friend. We agreed to keep things casual, but our conversations were always more intimate than we signed up for. I would often vent to him about family problems, the issues I was facing at work, and other things, to which he would always respond, "You'll be fine, you're strong." When I moved to Bed-Stuy in June 2020, in the midst of Black Lives Matter protests occurring every day, looting taking place in Manhattan, and a series of fireworks blasting off every evening until early morning throughout Brooklyn, I told Ian that I was beginning to get scared. I was scared to take the train alone, scared to get into an Uber alone, scared to leave my house. The racial tension in America was at a tremendous high and there were numerous stories floating around about missing Black women and random physical attacks occurring on the streets. One night, around 11 p.m., I called Ian and asked him if I could sleep over because the fireworks outside my window were keeping me awake. He told me he was at a friend's house, looking over a treatment, and that he wouldn't be home for another hour, without really inviting me to come by after. I was annoyed because I felt like if I had made it about sex, he would have asked me to come by after, as he had so many times before when I would hit him up during work. Or maybe he would have offered for me to come to where he was, while he finished working. But I tried to give him the benefit of the doubt. Maybe he really *was* busy. Maybe he and this friend needed to turn in this project proposal first thing in the morning. Possibly he had plans with another woman. But then, right before the call ended, Ian made a comment that led me to believe it wasn't just his busyness that stopped him from letting me sleep over. With complete certainty in his tone, he said, "You'll be fine, Bri, you're a strong Black woman. You shouldn't let these things scare you." But these things did scare me. It was often that I would vent to him about how uncomfortable the racial climate in America was making me feel, and each time he found a way to make me feel like my fears were a sign of weakness. Despite being a woman he was dating, someone he did genuinely care about and had spent a lot of time with, he didn't view me as a woman who needed his help or support. To Ian, I was a strong Black woman. I was fine. I had no reason to be afraid. I could, and should, look out for myself.

I stopped seeing Ian shortly after this conversation. I was too exhausted by all of the news surrounding BLM, my reporting on the racial climate, and educating random people on social media to find the energy to explain to Ian that I felt as if he had simplified my feelings to a trope. In that moment, I realized most of the men I had dated frequently expected me to act as a superhuman in situations when I would voice feeling afraid or unsafe. It sucked even more to realize that needing to advocate for myself wasn't only something present in healthcare settings or the workplace, but also existed within my relationships. Too many young Black women like myself have experienced this disregard for our fears and worries and are instead told that we are strong or will be fine. Almost as if we are supreme beings, capable of powering through any and every hardship. Actually, as if we are gods.

In 2017 a plethora of I MET GOD, SHE'S BLACK shirts were spotted on the backs of various celebrities. A fan of the phrase, I ordered one for myself. I almost ordered a matching poster to hang above my bed—so glad I didn't. Mostly because the perception I hold about Black women being compared to God was not the same idea that Dylan Chenfeld, the artist, held. Upon my research, I found that the artist is a self-described Jewish atheist who was always asking questions about what God is really like during his childhood. In an interview with *HuffPost*, Chenfeld said the idea was a way to poke fun at sacred cows, stating, "I'm taking the idea that God is a white male and doing the opposite of that, which is a black woman." When he first started printing the shirts, Chenfeld says most of the consumers were white. I, too, noticed white men mostly on Instagram donning the shirts. From the shirt's origin to the influx of white people buying it, it began to feel more like a controversial joke than a political statement or actual belief. Even one of my exes bought the shirt, telling me it was his way of showing people that he thought "Black girls were hot."

Whatever the case might be for why someone wants to wear a shirt that says I MET GOD, SHE'S BLACK, in my opinion, Black women *are* godly beings. The sun quite literally causes our skin to glisten as opposed to burning easily, and gravity has no control over how our hair falls. To some people, Black women might be godlike because they solve the world's problems and in the process sacrifice their own sanity for the sake of others. Like Jesus, or God, it's assumed that Black women can handle anything and everything, no matter the physical, mental, or emotional toll it might take on them. From our historical role as caregivers and nannies to white families to our modern-day portrayal as women who save democracy and defy the odds in our achievements, our spiritual and attentive nature is often mistaken as our societal role to take care of others. While we often do take on the burdens of the world and provide solutions and fixes, more often our offering goes unnoticed, and rarely does it translate into support from the ones we help.

When Jorge Guajardo, a Mexican politician and diplomat, tweeted, "Black women will save the United States," in regard to the 2020 election, collective agreement among others on Twitter suggested Democrats truly believed the fate of American politics fell on the shoulders of Black women voters. This expectation exists partly because the majority of Black women voters in the US vote Democratic (in 2020 about 90 percent of Black women voted for President-elect Joe Biden), but also because Black women would once again be the most affected by the racist ideology and conservative practices spewed and upheld by Donald Trump throughout his presidency. If Obamacare is demolished, Black women, who suffer more from diabetes, uterine fibroids, high blood pressure, and pregnancy complications, will not have the resources to treat those conditions. With sexual assault allegations and a history of publicly degrading women, Trump was not an appropriate choice for Black women, who are more likely to encounter sexual and domestic violence than any other demographic. Black women are the fastest-growing part of the prison population and endure a harder time finding housing than white women with criminal histories upon their release from prison. In addition to being the most unemployed group of women, more likely to act as the sole provider of their households, and having higher chances of living below the poverty line, Black women were not interested in being governed by one of the world's wealthiest men, who has been accused countless times of not paying taxes. All of this to say, Black women make up only 3.6 percent of all members of Congress and 3.7 percent of all state legislators, speaking directly to the lack of support Black women have in governing bodies. As a result, Black women were more likely to vote Trump out, organize, and show up to the booths at all, because we had more to lose should he have won. Since our livelihood is often at stake when political decisions do not lean toward the left, there is almost a biological response for Black women to fight for democracy whenever it's in danger. After witnessing the harmful effects that four years under Donald Trump had on American society—like increases in racial division, hate crimes, and right-wing hate speech on social media—Black women voting-rights activists began organizing with the hope that history would not repeat itself during the 2020 election. LaTosha Brown, the cofounder of the voting-rights group Black Voters Matter; Nsé Ufot, CEO of the New Georgia Project; and Stacey Abrams, a former member of the Georgia House of Representatives and founder of the New Georgia Project—all Black women—have been credited with helping turn Georgia blue for the first time in twenty-eight years, which to many was an act of God, a miracle.

Prior to the 2020 election, Brown's organization invested in more than six hundred Black-led groups on the ground. Before Biden took office, Ufot's nonpartisan group registered and engaged traditionally underrepresented Georgia voters in the civic process. After realizing Georgia's history of voting Republican could be offset if more minority voters were registered to vote, Abrams began mobilizing a team. Her crew knocked on two million doors, sent three million text messages, and made five million phone calls. In just two years, eight hundred thousand more Georgians were registered to vote. In 2020 she wrote a manual, *The Abrams Playbook*, detailing the tactics needed to flip red states blue. The advice proved successful when Pennsylvania, Wisconsin, and Michigan became swing states that November. When news broke that Georgia had turned blue, the internet thanked Black women for "saving American democracy" and, more specifically, for doing the work that others were not willing to take on themselves. Had it not been for the nearly 90 percent of Black woman voters who supported Joe Biden, America would have entered another four-year contract with Donald Trump. Time and time again, Black women prove to be the country's most powerful political force.

The 2020 presidential election was not the first time Americans at large benefited from the unpaid labor and organizing of Black women activists. From the women's suffrage movement to Stonewall and more recently the Black Lives Matter and #MeToo movements, Black women in America have a history of leading radical and social justice movements that immensely overshadow their efforts. Considering Black women are the Democratic Party's most loyal and dependable voting bloc, it's astounding to see the ways in which our vote has never been prioritized in American history. Dating back to the women's suffrage movement, Black women have been systematically and overtly discriminated against in a movement that outrageously benefited from their efforts, but more on that in the next chapter. Given all of this, it's clear to me that Black women are heroes who do not wear capes or receive credit for our heroism. From existing at the bottom of the social hierarchy to being the most mistreated in several areas of life, it makes me wonder how a society grapples with neglecting a group of people they so often verbally thank for "saving humanity." Why does gratitude never expand beyond lip service when concerning Black women?

Many Black women writers have taken it upon themselves to expose the twisted, unreciprocated beneficial relationship Black women hold with America. As Taylor Crumpton, a freelance culture writer, noted in her *Washington Post* piece "Black Women Saved the Democrats. Don't Make Us Do It Again," "Every four years, the Democratic Party looks to me and countless Black women to save it. Our White women counterparts aren't held to the same standard, especially not the 53 percent of them who voted for Trump in 2016. White women are granted forgiveness for their 'infidelity,' and wooed all over again each election, while Black women are expected to remain loyal and faithful." For *The Root*, Ashley Nkadi argued in her piece "Y'all Don't Deserve Black Women" that Black women are the unknown, original leaders of political stances that are later accepted by a wider audience. "Every time there is something good in this world—know that Black women probably did it first, said it first, seent it first," Nkadi wrote. "Conversely, most negative things in this world, Black women tried to save you from." In a piece titled "Black Women Are a Political Organizing Force. They're Not Unicorns," *HuffPost* writer Julia Craven explored the grassroots organizing Black volunteers in Alabama did to mobilize for Democratic senator Doug Jones. Craven emphasized the hard work and exhaustion that comes from such rallying, and the commonality of this responsibility falling on Black women. By ignoring the pain and depletion that comes with such labor, she wrote, non-Black people were playing into a "Magical Negro" stereotype.

The Magical Negro is a Black character who really seems to have no goal in life other than helping white people achieve their fullest potential; she may even be ditched or killed outright once she has served that purpose. In Hollywood, as in politics, the Magical Negro, or the comparison of Black women to unicorns and gods, is a righteous Black character whose only goal is to better the lives of white people and asks nothing for herself or her community. In film, her efforts are often related to fictional supernatural powers, and in real life, it's assumed she is born with inherent strength, directly superhumanizing her existence. While she is frequently praised for the advantages she has provided for white people, praised for her resilience and selflessness, she is too little acknowledged for the blood, sweat, and tears that went into securing the positive outcome.

A description on tvtropes.org describes the Magical Negro as someone "enlightened and selfless" and holding "no desire to gain glory for himself; he only wants to help those who need guidance . . . which *just happens* to mean those who are traditionally viewed by Hollywood as better suited for protagonist roles, not, say, his own oppressed people. If he does express any selfish desires, it will only be in the context of helping the white protagonists realize their own racism and thereby become better people." From Viola Davis in *Beautiful Creatures*, where she plays a magical mammy/librarian whose only purpose and desire in life is to help the white characters solve their problems, to Kat Graham's character, Bonnie Bennett, in *The Vampire Diaries*, to an unnamed elderly Jamaican woman in *Meet Joe Black* who has magical powers to see Joe for his true self and offers him advice about how to handle his tough situations, Black women as the Magical Negro is too common a trope in film. It's a white man's creation, fed to society to excuse the unreciprocated relationship between white need and Black support. Too often people come into Black women's lives and leave with far more than they had. Meanwhile, Black women are left with nothing. As Talesha Wilson, a Black feminist and activist, so eloquently laid out in a series of tweets:

> Too often, Black women get the short end of the sticks. And too often we're bullied into being satisfied with that. They tell us shit like "you doing too much," "stop rushing," "your expectations are too high," "you gotta see the potential." No the fuck we don't.

I want Black women to live a life that doesn't require a person to break us down to our smallest selves before realizing the MAGIC that's right in front of them. This goes for all relationships (platonic, romantic, work, family, and community) . . .

Black women are not the world's superhuman. We're not responsible for the adults around us. We don't have to stay anywhere that isn't serving us in the individual ways we need for any extended time.

Given our challenges, and our ability to persevere, dating from as far back as African slavery in America to the modern slavery of mass incarceration and police brutality, it is assumed by white America that Black people can overcome all things. Many of our ancestors have been fed the worst food, been provided no healthcare, endured the worst physical damage and beatings, worked outdoors in blazing temperatures, and denied proper education. Due to environmental racism, we lack access to healthy and affordable food options and are more likely to live in highly polluted neighborhoods that expose us to toxic waste and lead poisoning. We are constantly blocked from buying homes and being approved for business loans that can help bring our communities out of poverty, yet today we live on as some of the most resilient, successful, and talented people in America. Black women continue to be the most neglected and disrespected women in America, but we continue to pioneer culture, change, and democracy. Instead of our given-the-worse-but-coming-out-on-top relationship with America being viewed as unacceptable and needing change, it's perceived as magical and standard. What more white people need to recognize is that they're doing more damage to Black women by cheering us on from the sidelines rather than adopting our practices and using their privilege to make changes for us, themselves, and others. I can confidently speak for most Black women in that we'd prefer payment for our time and our efforts rather than empty praise, but the white liberal agenda focuses far too much on the idea of unity led by a white savior rather than equity afforded to the actual leader. Maybe it is our strength in numbers and drive that creates this expectation from others that we will bear the burdens of the world and create better circumstances for everyone else. If white liberals were to focus more on appropriating the political efforts and community organizing regarding social equality that Black women so often lead, as opposed to appropriating our style, expressions, and vernacular, maybe the just world they claim to want to create could actually exist.

The perception of Black women as providers, advisers, saviors, and ultimately heroes also stems from dependent practices white people implemented during slavery. Aside from relieving white women of their household duties, Black female slaves were expected to care for the children of their slave owners and aid white wives and children in times of illness. From preparing meals that kept the white slave owner family fed to bathing them before bed, Black women have historically acted as the caretakers of the white household. Even Black male slaves were expected to defend their master's home if it were ever attacked, and to provide safety for their slave owner's family. Enslavement of Black people in general is what created wealth, and later generational wealth, for white families. Their survival and advancement depended on the work, aid, and support of Black men, women, and children. When slavery was abolished, many Black women still served white families in exchange for little to no pay. Under the new guise of the help or the maid, Black women continued providing for white men and women by single-handedly raising their children, keeping their home intact, doing their shopping, and preparing their meals. White life depended on the efforts of Black women as much as white democracy depends on Black women organizers. Historically, white Americans have always relied on the work and disadvantages of others to advance their own ends, and as a result, the motivation to create change themselves, or a better world for others, in the ways that others have been forced to provide for them, can be foreign to them. A community that has little experience with America being a place of surviving the harms inflicted upon them by others is the exact kind of community that believes the ability to overcome systematic challenges is something magical. But minority communities in America, which have had no choice but to organize, create mutual aid, and mobilize in order to survive the paralyzations of white supremacy, know there is nothing magical about it.

For too many white Americans, Black people having super-human attributes and abilities is real, and the belief ultimately leads to greater abuse, reduced compassion, and an overall estrangement. It results in Black people being viewed as less sensitive to pain than white people in medical environments and Black hospital patients receiving less pain medication than whites. In a 2014 study, "A Superhumanization Bias in Whites' Perceptions of Blacks," white participants reported that Black people were more likely to have superhuman thick skin; to suppress hunger and thirst; to have supernatural quickness; and to have supernatural strength, further proving that some white Americans superhumanize Black people relative to white people.

The fantasy-driven differences that white people have imagined between the two races not only leave Black people more susceptible to inadequate healthcare, but also put us at higher risk in situations involving law enforcement. Although Black women account for 13 percent of women in the United States, they make up 20 percent of the women fatally shot by the police and 28 percent of unarmed killings. There are viral videos to prove it. Dajerria Becton was just fifteen years old when she survived a violent arrest during a friend's pool party. Breonna Taylor was only twenty-six years old when she was fatally shot in her Louisville, Kentucky, apartment by a police officer. Police use excessive force against Black girls and women frequently, and without just cause, just as they do to Black boys and men. In the aforementioned pepper-spraying of a nine-year-old Black girl by Rochester police, multiple full-grown adult white police officers can be seen dragging the girl into a car and heard mocking her for being afraid. At one moment, the girl yells, "Please don't do this to me," and a female officer responds, "You did it to yourself, hon." The little girl also tells police that her handcuffs are too tight and that her eyes are burning from the pepper spray, to which an officer responds, "If you stick your head towards the window, the cold air is going to feel nice." When the little girl says it's still burning too bad, the officer responds, "It's supposed to burn. It's called pepper spray." Throughout the entire encounter, the nine-year-old girl is trying not only to humanize herself, but also to make this group of adults realize that she poses no threat. After all, she is unarmed, one person, and smaller than all of them, but superhumanization bias fogs the perception entirely.

In April 2021, Ma'Khia Bryant, a sixteen-year-old Black girl, was fatally shot by an officer outside her home after she called the police for help. In the bodycam video, Bryant appears to be fighting with another girl and holding a knife. The officer shouts "Get down!" three times, pulls out his gun and shoots in Bryant's direction at least four times. She falls to the ground. One man standing off to the side on the driveway shouts to the officer, "She's just a kid!" That is the power superhumanization bias holds, the ability to turn a small child into a threatening opponent who can only be stopped with excessive force, or in many cases, death.

In "A Superhumanization Bias in Whites' Perceptions of Blacks," researchers Adam Waytz, Kelly M. Hoffman, and Sophie Trawalter write of superhumanization bias that "a subtler form of dehumanization of blacks persists [that] increases endorsement of police brutality against blacks... and reduces altruism toward blacks." A 2012 study conducted by the Malcolm X Grassroots Movement found that every twenty-eight hours in America, a Black person was a victim of an extrajudicial killing—defined as "killing by police that happens without trial or any due process." The perceived superhumanized strength that we hold as Black people, coupled with a belief that we are criminal and violent, shows how unconscious and implicit bias can alter the thought process during interactions between white and Black people and can lead people to react forcefully during calm situations.

Aside from medical environments and encounters with law enforcement, superhumanization can damage perceptions in relationships and friendships involving Black women and others. There have been several moments where superhumanization resulted in little to no support from my friends and colleagues, during rough times that would have caused the average person to crack. When I was let go from my media job and feared how I would manage to make ends meet in

New York City, an ex-coworker's last words to me were "You'll be fine, you're a resilient woman." That wasn't what I needed to hear at the time. I would have preferred her passing along any contacts she had. During the racial reckoning of summer 2020, when I spent most of my days balancing my full-time job and writing articles about social justice, and my nights scrolling through my Twitter feed full of police brutality videos, instead of offering support, my white friends asked for more information, thanked me for the articles I wrote that educated them, and gleefully invited me to attend protests as if they were social outings. I didn't need shallow invites to protests that I wouldn't be safe at but existed as a photo op for my friends; I needed a gift card for a massage, food ordered to my house, a simple curated playlist to take my mind off the trauma porn I was consuming. I needed money for therapy, or five dollars sent to my Venmo in the morning so I could grab coffee to fuel me through the day of putting together more resources for people like them to learn from. That summer I became the Magical Negro for many of my friends. Through my writing, I amplified the voices of dozens of Black people, educated white people, and created literature for those who were "listening and learning" to send to others. While I was paid for this work, of course, through the publications, not once did any of my white friends recognize the emotional and physical toll this nonstop, long-form trauma writing during a racial crisis and a global pandemic had on my mental and physical well-being. What they were able to recognize was that the pieces were helping them. I was their

Magical Negro, putting in hours day after day for the purpose of educating them in ways their own parents and schoolteachers never had, and for that, they thanked me via text message, on Instagram, on Twitter, or not at all. But thanking me on social media didn't change anything in my circumstances. If they were really consuming my work, they would have implemented my practices, Black practices, communal practices, into their own lives. They read my words about the harmful effects microaggressions and seeing Black bodies murdered on TV and on the internet have on the Black psyche but continued to probe me with long-winded questions and share bodycam videos on their social media accounts. They read my words about how tiring it is to educate white people throughout the course of our entire lives, yet most of them did not once ask me how I was doing. When searching for the word *strong* in my text messages, I came to realize that that summer I was told I was strong nearly forty different times. When I read one of my articles to a crowd of nearly four hundred white people at McCarren Park in Brooklyn, the same sentiment was expressed to me when the vigil ended. "You're so strong." "Your work has really educated me." "I've sent your article to my racist family members." The people I was doing so much for, who my work, my words, were doing so much for, did not once ask me, "What can I do for you?"

As I've gotten older, my relationship with being referred to as *strong* has changed. I once saw it as a compliment, or a personality trait that placed me above others. Other times I saw it as an obligation, or a duty to uphold a positive narrative for women like me. But recently, I've developed discontent with the characterization. After being told I was strong during exceedingly tough moments, I realized that I was expected to power through and was rarely offered support because of this expectation. I was expected to get through things alone, as if the obstacles in my life, which were completely out of my control, were viewed as life lessons. If I could choose, I wouldn't have to be strong, but the obstacles and struggles faced by Black women like me allow me no other choice. If I'm not strong, I'll fail. If I'm not strong, I'll fall behind. If I'm not strong, who will be strong for me? Even when I'm questioning myself about why I am uncomfortable with being strong—something that many people claim to aspire to be, flash as something to flex—the tweets of several other people remind me that the expectation for us to be strong isn't normal, and once again, I feel seen.

I dream of never being called resilient again in my life. I'm exhausted by strength. I want support. I want softness. I want ease. I want to be amongst kin. Not patted on the back for how well I take a hit. Or for how many.

I taught mostly Black kids in Oakland and people always talked about how resilient they were as a way to excuse why white ppl in charge just let them live with racism and poverty without caring.

Something has always bothered me about #resilient. We talk about . . . resilience without examining the system of #whitesupremacy and #oppression that requires #resilience in order to survive what has been designed to oppress.

When my friend Maxine posted a video on YouTube about why Black women shouldn't have to be strong, and questioned why the phrase *strong white woman* doesn't exist, I became more aware of the lack of strength white women, and other non-Black women, are expected to possess. In a world that caters to whiteness, that protects, believes, and hears white women more than any other women, such strength is not necessarily needed. But in a world of accumulated inequalities like racial inequality; social, political, and economic exclusion; and medical underservice, Black women *do* actually have to fend for themselves. In providing for ourselves and looking out for ourselves, a new stereotype occurred: the strong Black woman, or as Hollywood often depicts, the Black superwoman. She's the single Black mother who is doing it all without any help. She doesn't complain about having no support, she doesn't seek it from those around her, and she refuses to let others, especially men, step in. She's content with being strong, even though viewers can see that it's killing her, slowly wearing her down.

It's a twisted trope, because while her struggles are obvious, her disinterest in asking for or receiving help and her ability to power through and sacrifice her own well-being is posed as oddly aspiring. Think of Precious in *Precious*, whose only aspiration is to be a good mother and care for someone else, despite all the harm inflicted upon her, or Michonne in *The Walking Dead*, who displays a grounded and encouraging spirit and possesses exceptional physical strength, yet she mostly ends up using these assets to repeatedly save the other characters, time and time again. Or think of Taraji P. Henson's character, Joss Carter, in *Person of Interest*, who exhibits a strong moral compass, is exceedingly professional, and seems to fear nothing, which equates to her being a valuable resource and readily available to the white protagonists in the series.

Maybe film and TV's frequent portrayal of Black women as strong has reinforced the belief among young Black women that strength is an attribute we should strive to embody. In a 2010 study titled "Superwoman Schema: African American Women's Views on Stress, Strength, and Health," Black women participants reported that the superwoman role had benefits like preservation of self and family or community and liabilities like relationship strain, stress-related health behaviors, and stress embodiment. Similar to burnout, the expectation to power through hardships, provide for others, and maintain composure has led Black women to endure great stress with little to no relief. According to Arline T. Geronimus, an American public health researcher and research professor, the aftermath is premature weathering. Her hypothesis found that the inequalities faced by Black women, historically and today, decrease access to resources and heighten susceptibility to psychological stress and premature stress-related illness. Then there's allostatic load, or "the wear and tear on the body," which accumulates as an individual is exposed to repeated or chronic stress. According to neuroendocrinologist Bruce Sherman McEwan and coauthor Huda Akil, chronic exposure to psychological stress leads to cumulative risk and physiological dysregulation (e.g., impaired cardiovascular, metabolic, immune, and neuroendocrine functioning), yielding chronic illness and premature mortality. These two societal factors provide an explanation for the health disparities between African American women and white American women.

The notion of Black women as superwomen was created partially as a result of African American women's efforts to counteract negative societal portrayals of African American womanhood—such as Mammy, Jezebel, Sapphire, and Welfare Queen—and to acknowledge unsung attributes that developed and continue to exist despite oppression and hardships. The specific obstructive experiences of Black women, including race- and gender-based oppression, disenfranchisement, and limited resources, during and after enslavement in America, coupled with the compromised and disenfranchised position of Black men, which limited their ability to provide financial and emotional support to their partners and families, forced many Black women to take on the roles of mother, nurturer, and breadwinner out of economic and social necessity. Ultimately, being a superwoman is not a choice; it's a necessity for survival and has created a multifaceted role that influences the ways that Black women experience and report stress. As R. E. Romero so eloquently noted about the strong Black woman phenomenon in "The Icon of the Strong Black Woman: The Paradox of Strength," "an overused asset that develops uncritically without ongoing evaluation and attention to changing needs and demands runs the risk of becoming a liability. 'Strong Black Woman' is a mantra for so much of U.S. culture that it is seldom realized how great a toll it has taken on the emotional well-being of the African American woman. As much as it may give her the illusion of control, it keeps her from identifying what she needs and reaching out for help."

The superwoman trope doesn't just leave Black women neglected and subject us to detrimental stress; it also causes us to associate our overwork with expectation, and therefore success. The Romero study found that the superwoman role leads to the obligation to manifest strength, the obligation to suppress emotions, a resistance to being vulnerable or dependent, the determination to succeed despite limited resources, and the obligation to help others. When speaking with my friends about the ways in which being strong has affected our relationships and well-being, many expressed an obligation to present an image of strength for the sake of their parents, other family members, and future children. Some felt they were perceived as "the strong friend" by their non-Black colleagues and peers and that they were expected to push through any obstacle that confronted them, even when others were likely to react with weakness in similar situations. One friend, who is a first-generation American, felt she needed to present an image of strength because there were other Black women in her family who had faced more challenges than she had, in migrating to America and leaving their previous life and home behind. Another friend, who was the first in her immediate family to attend college, felt the same pressure because she was the family's "meal ticket out of poverty." Among my group of Black woman friends, how strong they felt they had to be varied by economic status and how long their family had been in America. Those who were the first to go to college, land a well-paying job, or move to a large city expressed that they were expected to be strong even when they didn't feel like doing so, while those who came from families with better resources or countries where women are highly supported by their spouse and community stated that they felt obligated to present an image of strength only at work. All of them, despite differences in upbringing and resources, agreed that the trope was harmful, and all of them were intentionally rejecting it. One friend, a twenty-six-year-old video producer in Brooklyn, said,

> I think Black women are looked at as these people that just make a way out of no way. It's expected that we're gonna figure it out, we're gonna accomplish our goals, without help from our families, partners, and community. People expect us not to crack under pressure and always deliver, and then praise our struggle and grind without realizing that most people

are in need of help when they're struggling and grinding. It's actually very weird when you think of the ways people strip the humanity from us and view us as this mythical creature that has superpowers to push through anything. I don't think women of other races deal with this issue, because just as we're thinking about the term *strong Black woman* you don't ever hear strong white women, right? You don't hear strong Asian women. It doesn't even sound normal to say. They're given this freedom to be like delicate, soft women. We're kind of taught as women that it's a feminine characteristic to be delicate. That women need help. That women are gonna cry and it's not shameful. But it's way more acceptable for non-Black women to do this because they don't have this stereotype and expectation looming over them of being strong and resilient.

I also spoke to older Black women, mostly in their late forties or well into their fifties, about presenting an image of strength, and their reasoning was different than that of my younger friends. Some shared that being strong was just part of womanhood and, specifically, Black womanhood. Others spoke with a sense of pride about manifesting an image of strength and viewed it as a characteristic others lacked and should strive to imitate. Despite the difference in age and generation, a common sentiment persisted: the widespread belief that Black women are strong and should power through hardships meant less support when it was really needed. While older Black women spoke in opposites and shared that being strong meant not being weak or frail, younger Black women expressed that being strong meant keeping things to yourself and at other times advocating for yourself. When I asked my friends if they viewed being called strong as a compliment or a dismissal, many of them responded with "both."

Graduate student, New York City, age twenty-six:

I think it's a mix, but I would still say that it's really hard to receive it as a positive, if anyone, other than another Black woman, is saying it. And even then it can be loaded. It's kind of in the same category as being called "articulate" or "exceptional." By definition, they're positive things, but the weight and the history associated with them is so heavy, that when somebody says it to you as a Black woman, you have to kind of question their intentions and what they mean by that. At the same time, they could be dismissing how difficult things are that you do and do well.

Journalist, Jersey City, age thirty-one:

I think it's a little of both, depending on the context. Ultimately the word *strong*, I believe, is a compliment, but it all depends on if you're connecting my strength with a certain trauma or something negative. Then it will lean into a dismissal, because I don't want to only be seen as strong if it's because I'm picking up the slack for something or because I've been through hell and back. That's not why I want to be strong. I want to be strong because I stand up for myself and am someone that has my life together, but not because the world is constantly throwing shit my way and expecting me to just deal with it.

Writer, Brooklyn, age thirty-four:

I really think the way we receive the trope varies based on the individual's upbringing, socioeconomic factors, and the class that they're in. A lot of people have been intentionally and consciously rejecting that sort of notion that brought them to need to be strong. I also know others, and sometimes these groups overlap, other people that are proud of it. I think for some people it has become a coping mechanism and maybe they don't have an awareness of how the trope harms them, as much as it maybe heals something for them. I don't think that as a community, or as communities of Black women, we really have the space and time and resources to really address superwoman schema and strong Black women theory and really unpack it to maybe keep the good things, but discard the really harmful ways that it hurts us physically, mentally, and spiritually.

Another friend, a twenty-seven-year-old medical school student in Dallas, Texas, didn't view it as a compliment at all and compared it to traits and attributes withheld for men:

> I see it completely as a dismissal. I think it plays into stereotypes that existed well before our time. In my opinion, when you say a woman is strong, oftentimes you can't be strong and feminine. Usually strong connotes a very masculine trait, or very masculine role. As a woman, you don't want to necessarily be portrayed as masculine. You don't want to be portrayed as rough or tough. And oftentimes, I believe strong is associated with those words. I believe the notion of being strong kind of extends back into slavery when Black women were on the fields, working, being beat and raped, and having their babies ripped away from them. They were strong in dealing with all of that. But when you are strong, you don't have room to be soft or tender or feminine, or more specifically, protected. Because you're strong, you can handle yourself. And so I think in many ways, it's why Black women are often not protected, especially when it comes to domestic violence or even cases of justice, murder and just general violence in the world.

One friend, a twenty-eight-year-old publicist in New York City, agreed that the trope leaves Black women unprotected and, ultimately, disbelieved:

Whenever I've tried to explain to non-Black people, or even Black men, how emotionally draining it is for me to have so many expectations on my shoulders, they literally don't understand a word coming out of my mouth. I feel like the experiences of Black women are so niche and individual to us that other people assume we are complaining or in our head about what we go through because they literally cannot relate to or even contextualize what we are talking about. They will just look at you like you're crazy, as if we are making things up.

It's common for Black women to feel that those with more privilege do not fully understand what they're going through, whether it be Black men in a patriarchal society or non-Black people who are positioned higher on the social hierarchy. It makes it more difficult to let people in, and more common to bottle up emotions and suppress discomfort. Even when someone is willing to listen, the conversation can often be draining because of the time and emotional effort it takes to explain and convince someone of a situation that they do not experience. And because there's already a high expectation for Black women to be strong and fend for themselves, sometimes just venting or sharing concerns is perceived as a sign of weakness. As one of my friends, a thirty-one-year-old editor in Los Angeles, stated, "Most of the time it just feels easier to suppress what we're feeling rather than involve someone else. But I guess that isn't a good solution, because where do all these frustrations go? Black women rarely get to process or work through the bullshit that is so often pushed on us, unless we're talking to other Black women or seeing a Black therapist."

As a result, we may become less vulnerable and dependent beings, and over time, it becomes hard for us to accept and seek help from others. We may learn to fear vulnerability and dependence because we fear it will result in us being hurt, disappointed, or gaslighted. Or we may assume that asking for support might cause others to think we are incapable, inadequate, or unwilling to handle things on our own. All these pressures, which often form from stereotypes completely out of our control and fictional narratives derived from propaganda created by white people, push Black women to constantly be superwomen. We feel an intense motivation to succeed despite limited resources, not only to prove people wrong, but also to create better conditions for those who will come after us, and for those we love. We don't bow down during times of adversity, and we do believe, in time, we can likely overcome any obstacle thrown in our way. Like my friends, I believe I can reach my goals even without having all the resources and support needed to do so, because I have seen countless Black women before me do it time and time again. The superwoman characteristics in those achievements are the late hours worked, sacrificed sleep, breaks not taken, and in some cases putting our health on the back burner to reach our goals. Because so many of us are the first in our families to attain certain educational and professional achievements, we cannot often rely on our family members to provide the extra boost of resources that other, more privileged individuals might have. So again, we are obligated to work harder, be ambitious, and overperform. For many of us, our strength is not just a characteristic; it's a legacy and duty that we must carry out because of the circumstances we are allotted.

Like many of my friends, I have been taught by my family to provide for myself, without the assistance of a spouse or support from external forces. While we are allowed to cry more often than our male counterparts, many of us are still told to be strong and pick ourselves up when displaying negative emotions. But many of us are starting to reject this model of resilience passed down from our ancestors and displayed to us in the media. As more Black women are embracing therapy and prioritizing their mental health, softness and delicate femininity are replacing the need for us to keep a "stiff upper lip" about the pain and obstacles we are subjected to. This trend of young Black women bucking the stereotypes of strength and resilience, and promoting their soft lifestyles via social media, is popularly known as the Soft Black Girl aesthetic. But the aesthetic is less of a social media trend concerned with beauty and more of a practice of rejecting white society's attempts to exclude Black women from femininity by labeling us as sassy, aggressive, and overly sexual beings. The Soft Black Girl trope dismantles these harmful stereotypes by displaying soft traits like gentleness, delicacy, and innocence, which are rarely associated with Blackness. It makes space for young Black women in an area that has long been thought of as exclusive to White and Asian women, making softness an act of rebellion, a rejection of harsh expectation, and the act of putting our well-being first.

As writer Evie Muir penned in an article for *Refinery29* on celebrating Soft Black Girl Summer, "Knowingly or not, this trend signifies an antithesis to the many stereotypical perceptions of misogynoir that define Black women by adjectives such as 'strong' and 'independent.' We're emboldened in our suffering yet taught we're less deserving of safety, peace, and love. We're to be pitied and saved—but also feared. More than just a soft aesthetic, this trend motivates us towards a soft lifestyle. One that focuses on relaxation, leisure pursuits, space to explore hobbies, unlocking our creativity and spending time in and around nature."

Black women deserve still moments and space to rest. As the superwomen of the world, the godlike beings who make the impossible seem possible, the unsung heroes who so often take charge during times of adversity, we are worthy of support and resources the same way our white women counterparts are granted grace for their discomforts, of all sizes. A world without Black women is a world without just leadership, inclusive practices, democracy, actual change, and progression, and if the world continues to neglect and abandon Black women's well-being, that is the world they will get.

CHAPTER 8

Woke

Prior to summer 2020, my main condition for the white people in my life was that they had to be woke. Whether they were friends or lovers, I was not interested in mingling with white people who didn't identify with the term. At the time, it took the bare minimum for me to label someone as such, like voting blue and being aware of white privilege, and many of my friends *loved* it. They loved being told they were woke by a Black person. It made them feel different from the white people they thought to be racist and separated them from "those white people" in conversations regarding white supremacy or tragedies inflicted by white people. But very soon, after the surge of the Black Lives Matter movement took over our summer and consumed our social media feeds, I realized that during some moment over the years, the word *woke* went from describing someone who is highly aware about the ways in which they perpetuate racism to someone who is a bit more realistic about racism than their peers. It didn't necessarily mean someone who makes space for or creates opportunities for those less privileged than them, but instead it meant something simpler, someone who is kind to others regardless of their skin color. Woke didn't mean someone who is anti-racist; it meant someone who isn't blatantly racist. It didn't mean someone who exhibits empathy for others' experiences; it meant someone who agrees those experiences shouldn't happen. Being "woke," before 2020, was simple. Too simple. And now it's become very apparent how little an effect placing the term on some people actually has on their actions.

Before *woke* meant something white people could be portrayed as, it meant something that Black people should be in order to survive in a racist climate. In 2017, *woke* was added to the Oxford English Dictionary as an adjective meaning "originally: well-informed, up-to-date. Now chiefly: alert to racial or social discrimination and injustice." But two years prior, Urban Dictionary, where most culturally Black terms are defined before hitting the mainstream, defined the term as "being aware...knowing what's going on in the community (related to racism and social injustice)." When author and journalist Leslie Streeter tweeted, "'Woke' was a term developed within the African-American community as a reminder to be aware and prepared. It was stolen to be directed at White people suspected of 'virtue signaling' as a way to disarm its power and pervert it. Using it as a pejorative tells on yourself," the change of the word's meaning caused me to reflect on who I had witnessed, in my own social circle, self-identify as woke, progressive, and liberal: one of my former white best friends who dates Republican guys she didn't feel comfortable bringing around me; an old boss who opposed me talking about Black Lives Matter at work; a guy I briefly dated who held such deep unconscious biases about me that he didn't find me suitable to have a relationship with until he found out I was about to land a book deal; a previous manager who refused to promote me or even acknowledge my triumphs because she always saw an unreasonable need for improvement; a friend who said she doesn't like to be *political* on social media when I asked her why she went silent on Instagram during summer 2020. And so many more. Streeter's tweet also caused me to reflect on which white people in my social circle I had bestowed the label upon: a friend who added BLM to her Instagram bio only to remove it weeks later, a guy who dated mostly Black women, a colleague who spoke of white people in the third person. None of these things actually meant these people were dismantling racism or doing active work to combat white supremacy, yet for some reason, I had been impressed by the simplest gestures.

And yet, events throughout 2020 revealed that these widespread simple gestures, especially digital ones, did not necessarily mean that the racial reckoning had resulted in widespread reformation. When social media platforms led by white influencers and creators began to center Black content during the summer of 2020, I was once again bamboozled into thinking we had entered a post-racial era. Predominantly white businesses publicly pledged to "do the work," Europeans overseas posted black squares to display solidarity with Black

Americans, the streets were filled with racially mixed crowds of people chanting "Black lives matter." Of course, for a moment, I, like many other liberals, believed a great awakening had led to a reformed nation. But just a couple of years later, the momentum surrounding racial justice online has died down, just as every trend on social media does once it outruns its cycle.

I don't knock the impact and influence that occurred during that summer of racial reckoning, but I also recognize the ways in which the conditions of Black Americans have not improved. We are still underpaid and underrepresented across industries. Black women are still dying at high rates from childbirth. We're still reporting bias and microaggressions to a large degree in our respective workspaces, social environments, and medical settings. We're still fearful that the next election will involve even more mobilizing and rallying on our part to keep Trump out of office in 2024. A fear that was stoked when the 2020 election results disclosed that Trump had maintained a large white vote in liberal hotbeds like New York (48 percent), California (47 percent), and Washington (36 percent). These numbers don't align with the national performance of white allyship online. So where was the blind spot that made it seem like white support for the same man who asked the Proud Boys to "stand back and stand by" had lessened?

Ultimately, social media has created a fake indicator of progress that simply involves acknowledging privilege publicly while privately ignoring it, working against it, or forgetting about it. It's easy to share a news clip or add a hashtag to your bio, and while that might grab people's attention, it doesn't really result in personal or structural change. It takes time, effort, and consistency to pull meaning from that news clip or hashtag and apply it to your day-to-day life—something many people are still unwilling to do.

Too often, white people equate their kindness to the ways in which they are *not* racist to others. In an op-ed titled "Dear White Women, Our Kindness Is Worthless," writer Kayla Wiltfong explores the dissociation some liberal white women often fall victim to when reflecting on the role they play in racism, pertaining to the 2020 election. "The kindness offered by white women means nothing, just as the notorious black square, a social media response to George Floyd's death, was nothing but performance. The bottom line is, there is a problem in white communities, and us white women are not carrying our weight," she writes, noting, "There's really no excuse for this kind of behavior. When it comes down to people's rights, kindness means nothing and action means everything. Whether or not we voted for Trump, at this point, is no matter; we need to do as much to mobilize our communities as Black women are doing. We cannot let our privilege blind us to the severity of the fight." Wiltfong's plea to her white sisters is the same plea Black people, especially Black women, have been asking white women to get on board with for centuries. And rightfully so, it can be hard to dismantle something when some people hold strong relationships with the same people carrying out the specific racism we are asking to dismantle. Most of my white friends have admitted to having racist grandparents, parents, cousins, or other family members. Some have racist friends and coworkers and have been in several situations where people confide their racist thoughts to them in the absence of Black people. And while they claim to not agree, they more than often agree to disagree, directly normalizing socializing with, loving, and maintaining relationships with people who are racist.

These same people would not agree to disagree about pedophilia or abuse of animals. But with racism, many white people choose to be complacent and have learned to still love and support those who have proven time and time again to be racist. In fact, 35 percent of Biden voters in 2020 reported they have a few close friends who supported Trump, the same man who refused to denounce white supremacy, lied about the severity of the pandemic, and was comfortably vocal about his sexist and misogynistic beliefs. It begged the question, were white liberals actually doing the groundwork their social media profiles portrayed? I've witnessed white women who call themselves liberal and allies go on to date and marry much more conservative, and sometimes racist, men. It speaks to some white people's ability to disassociate themselves from their own history and, furthermore, truth. So often, even the "kind" white people embolden racists by their complicity in silence and tolerance. When self-identified liberal white people agree to set aside differences with family members, friends, and romantic partners—differences that quite literally contribute to the systemic issues liberals claim to want to dismantle—it aligns these two people more than they'd like to admit. It aligns them in complacency toward issues that ultimately don't have a significant effect on their well-being. Does it stem from the ability to be more accepting of others' political views? Or maybe having mastered the art of compartmentalization? Or is it simply that self-interest outweighs having the integrity to support a cause even though it doesn't negatively impact your conditions? What does it tell us about the impact, inner workings, and true beliefs of self-professed liberals who behave in ways that don't align with what they claim to stand for? A true ally, someone who is actually "woke," would not tolerate racist behavior to any degree or of any kind. Instead, they would have hard conversations with the people in their lives and call them out when they are wrong. They won't forgive them for things that do not directly affect them, without seeing change occur. They wouldn't consider themselves saviors while detaching themselves from pressing issues affecting Black people today, or prioritize the maintenance of a progressive digital aesthetic over actual action and reform. Beyond that, they would take cues from Black women, Black people, without asking us to carry their burden time and time again. They would organize white Democratic voters for important elections, the same way they continuously see Black women do. They would decenter themselves and not view solidarity from them as something earned rather than something deserved.

Imani Barbarin, a disabled activist, once said in a TikTok video, "White people never miss an opportunity to remind you that their solidarity with you is optional. If you're not nice while asking for it, they have the option to tap out. Racism for them is a special interest; racism for you is your life." To that Chivona Renée Newsome, co-founder of Black Lives Matter Greater New York, added, "Talks of unity are used to make us complacent. Just like equality, it is a myth. Equity is what's needed. I demand uninterrupted access to the 'American Dream' for my People."

I've witnessed firsthand how talk surrounding unity is often just a self-fulfilling prophecy that many white people use to appear to be peacemakers or to offer quick solutions to a complex issue. For example, during the summer of "listening and learning" many white influencers took to Instagram and called upon their followers to unite and spread peace, kindness, and love, as opposed to sharing the harms that were being projected to the world. In this call for unity, the unspoken request is silence. It was a tactic to stop people from talking about the problem, because it made said influencer uncomfortable, or took the spotlight from their platform. Any unity that requires someone to stay silent is not unity at all. However, it *is* repressing someone's voice. Suggesting we all come together while shutting down conversation or attention to a topic that brings light to an issue is a deflection and doesn't center the people who need advocacy. It is not being an ally—but rather the complete opposite. It gaslights the messenger and discounts the detriment of the issue all while claiming that it's done in good faith and that it's a better solution.

Allies of Black women must understand that their support of Black women online is truly productive when it reflects their behavior offline. Social media creates a space for people to feel as if they are doing concrete work by letting a few posts equate to making lifestyle changes. We must ask, have I done work within my own social circles or used my privilege to make space for Black women at work? Have I offered any opportunities to Black women? Have I sponsored a Black woman in any way? Have I loaned my platform to a Black woman who could better educate their followers than a solid black square?

What causes many people to believe that unity or simple notions of togetherness are solutions to solving racism and creating a more just world for Black people? Perhaps the idea that we live in a post-racial society has blurred the lines. When Barack Obama became the first Black president of the United States, when Kamala Harris was sworn in as the first Black vice president, when Derek Chauvin, a white former police officer, was convicted of the murder of George Floyd, when Nancy Pelosi appeared on Capitol Hill wearing kente stoles, many liberals were repeatedly convinced that we were living in a post-racial society. But the belief that infrequent wins equate to a cured society built on a foundation of oppression is dangerous. With this belief, it convinces many liberals that conditions for Black people—everyday Black people, Black people without social or celebrity status, without wealth—have greatly improved. But that simply isn't the case.

Obama becoming president didn't cure racism; in fact, many people were so upset and shocked by the fact that a Black man was able to earn such a position that they voted to replace him with a businessman with no political background and a history of racist, misogynist, and sexist rhetoric. Having the first Black woman vice president didn't stop lawmakers from pushing forward a ban on abortion, which will mostly impact Black women. Derek Chauvin's conviction had no effect on the outcomes of fairness in the justice system when Kyle Rittenhouse was found not guilty of any charges.

In a 2015 article for *The Atlantic* titled "There Is No Post-Racial America," author Ta-Nehisi Coates dives into the myth of post-racial America by describing *post-racial* as a term that is never used in earnest and often used by journalists attempting to measure improvement in race relations post-Obama. He writes, "The Obama-era qualifier is also inherently flawed, because it assumes that the long struggle that commenced when the first enslaved African arrived on American soil centuries ago could somehow be resolved in an instant, by the mere presence of a man who is not a king." What I've come to notice is that the only people asking me if I agree that things are getting better are people who have the best conditions. It is the people who are not fighting for their own civil rights who seem to believe that there has been immense improvement in the living conditions of Black people since inequality is no longer as blatant as a WHITES ONLY sign on the front door of a shop. But if you just pay attention—to the data, to the rhetoric, to the response—when Black people seek justice, seek to be treated as equals, as human beings, the system that promises liberty and justice actually is for "whites only."

In a patriarchal world that still mostly proves to support, aid, center, and humanize whites only, to a much greater capacity, it is white women who hold power in creating equal conditions. Similar to Wiltfong stating that white women are not carrying their weight, and other literature surrounding race and privilege asking more of white women, I've put more emphasis on the responsibility of white women as allies as opposed to their white male counterparts. Because white women do hold a marginalized identity—their gender—it is more likely, or expected, that they will vote in the interest of, support, and act as allies to other women, and people of marginalized identities. But that isn't always how it plays out. White men and women mostly date and marry homogeneously, and it is not uncommon for white women to vote differently than the men they lie next to. But, in my experience, a liberal Black woman, who is on the opposite side of the privilege scale from white men, is far less likely to enter a romantic relationship with a conservative white man who votes red, because the policies he supports directly impact her community.

In a 2020 article for *The Guardian*, I interviewed Gwen Kansen, a self-identified liberal white woman who briefly dated a Proud Boy. The man's "phone screensaver was of Pepe the Frog—a symbol of the alt-right movement. His style reminded her of a Confederate soldier, and he wore badges proudly proclaiming his hatred for political correctness," yet Kansen still found him attractive, so much that she entertained the idea of dating him. Whether white women continue to love and befriend white men who do not agree with them politically and socially because the disagreement doesn't have a detrimental effect on their well-being, or because they hold their love interests to lower standards regarding anti-racism, it is their bond with white men that provides them the upper hand in reaching them, educating them, and pulling them away from upholding white supremacist ideology and practices.

I would never knowingly go on a date with a Proud Boy, or even a man who holds racist beliefs, but it is not nearly as uncommon for white women, who have normalized these behaviors and character flaws and often make exceptions for them. I think it's equally safe to assume that most of the straight white men who will pick up this book and read it will have done so only after it was recommended by a white woman they love, trust, or care about. We've witnessed how white people, especially white men, will ignore the pleas of Black people, especially Black women, until another white person has repeated the same plea to them. As humans, we are wired to offer attention to those we find attractive, and we equate attractiveness with worth. White men, who highly regard white women as attractive, are more likely to hear their pleas than a Black woman's. Take the mainstream attention

Black women's lives received in summer 2020 as an example. It wasn't the first time Black people lost their lives to police brutality, and it most definitely wasn't the first time that Black people posted about it online, shared their stories to their social media feeds, and demanded attention from their white counterparts. However, it wasn't until there was widespread attention from white people that other white people finally took an interest in these tragedies. It wasn't enough to see their Black friend on Instagram post about Alton Sterling, Philando Castile, or Stephon Clark years before. It was witnessing people who looked like them, people they found to be important and valued, other white people, white women, posting about these tragedies that finally garnered their undivided attention. The reality is that the majority of elected officials, CEOs, and industry leaders in America are white men, which makes the pressure on white women to not only educate themselves but ensure the white men in their lives are being educated continuously more pressing. I think a lot of white women feel like doing the work for themselves is enough, while overlooking the reality that most men will not share the same initiative or "come to it in their own time."

Black women put more responsibility on white women to both support Black women and check their white male counterparts because at one point in history, they, too, were not offered the same rights as their white male counterparts. We figure that because white women also experience sexual assault, earn less pay, are subjected to unfair abortion laws, are offered inadequate maternity leave, and deal with glass ceilings and negative stereotypes associated with their gender, they would naturally feel motivated to create more just environments for themselves and other women, or understand the pleas of Black women. But that is not always the case. Regardless of intersectional identities, whiteness often practices self-preservation. In situations where white people hold intersectional identities or marginalized identities, oftentimes they are used to separate them from whiteness. What some white people with these other identities struggle with, when making their case for why they are not like "other whites," is that they *are* still white, still benefit from being white, and still navigate through a society that sees their race before any other identity they might hold. It seems that recently, as whiteness has become something frowned upon by the Left, some liberal white people have become so hell-bent on not identifying as white that they completely overlook breaking down the systems that uphold their privilege of being white or white-passing. This self-separation can unconsciously be used as a tool to other themselves and not relate to the wrongdoings by white people at large, rather than actually do work that will help create more just conditions and treatment for others. This topic is hard to explore in the mainstream, and for many reasons. Oftentimes discussing whiteness that is tied to marginalized identities causes the person in that group to feel their struggles are being undermined or gaslighted. But that is not the case, and I think many people with marginalized identities, who are simultaneously white, understand this. But the frustration with still fitting an identity that is highly privileged, and the power that privileged identity has in lessening their marginalized struggle, is what many people are not ready to reckon with. As a Black woman, when explaining my hardships to white women, I have often been met with responses like, "I get it, I'm a woman too." But what *I* am describing is my niche experience as a woman who is also Black, which increases my exposure to whatever the harm might be and lessens my ability to receive support or defend myself.

Consider the maternal mortality rate in America. For all women, giving birth in the United States is a dangerous risk, given that the country has higher rates of maternal deaths than forty-five other countries and is the only developed country with a consistently rising maternal mortality rate. But that rate increases when you're a Black woman. Just in New York City, Black women are twelve times more likely to die from pregnancy-related complications than white women. So as a Black woman, when explaining my struggles to white women about maternal mortality, I am not interested in hearing that they can relate, because actually, they cannot relate to having the highest maternal mortality. Instead, I want to hear how our shared gender identity, coupled with their privilege as white women, is going to be used to change the outcomes for Black women who are not afforded the same conditions.

During the summer of 2020, my friend and fellow model Khrystyana Kazakova shared her modeling agency's Instagram platform with me to discuss how to be a better ally. Not only was I paid for my time, I was given the spotlight to share this knowledge instead of having it overshadowed by someone who might have gained the knowledge from me and other Black women. Before this book was even a proposal, my white friend Leah Fessler introduced me to a few literary agents who had previously approached her about writing a book. All of them offered to work with me, and although I didn't move forward with her contacts, I was appreciative of her sharing her network with me, especially given that Black woman writers are greatly overlooked in publishing. Also, during a doctor's visit that involved various forms of uncomfortable tests to decide on a diagnosis, my friend Brittany Lince—also a white woman, who was originally joining for emotional support—advocated for me when the technician and doctor continuously ignored my pain. Brittany took it into her own hands to order the technician to stop the testing and threatened to report the situation, but most important, she offered to accompany me to my following appointments because she understood that the bias that often results in medical professionals neglecting Black patients meant that those same medical professionals were more likely to listen to her. This is the work of true allies, who are willing to extend their resources and support to other women who are often overlooked.

In the fight for equality between genders, which in most cases is a fight for equality between white men and white women, some white women have labeled themselves as progressives

and abolitionists without considering forming better outcomes for other women in the process. While white women
have played an integral role in many social justice movements,
history shows that a lot of white feminist work has been exclusive rather than intersectional. Historically, white feminist
movements, like the suffrage movement, often neglected obtaining equal conditions for non-white women, and followed
practices similar to those created by white men, from whom
these white women claimed to be taking back the power.

When white women's suffrage activists like the highly
praised Susan B. Anthony and Elizabeth Cady Stanton
learned that working alongside their African American
women counterparts was opposed by white Southerners, anti-
Black rhetoric and actions were employed to further the support of only white women obtaining the right to vote. These
women did not work to prioritize making voting rights accessible to all women and even publicly denounced Black male
suffrage—which Black women explicitly supported. While
American history books and lectures commend white suffragists like Anthony as pioneers and leaders of the women's
suffrage movement—even issuing her own dollar in 1979—her
legacy involved fighting to ensure Black men didn't get the
vote before white women, and indirectly advancing white supremacy.

When Anthony and Stanton cofounded *Revolution*, a
women's rights newspaper, they accepted funding from
George Francis Train, a Democrat who supported slavery.
When publicly discussing the Fifth Amendment, rhetoric

closely aligned with white supremacist values was often spewed by white woman suffragists. Anthony went so far as to say she'd cut off her right arm before asking for the ballot for Black men; Anna Howard Shaw, president of the National American Woman Suffrage Association, argued that "you have put the ballot in the hands of your black men, thus making them political superiors of white women. Never before in the history of the world have men made former slaves the political masters of their former mistresses!" Rebecca Ann Latimer Felton, the first woman to serve in the Senate, pushed a dangerous message surrounding lynching Black voters: "I do not want to see a negro man walk to the polls and vote on who should handle my tax money, while I myself cannot vote at all," she said. "When there is not enough religion in the pulpit to organize a crusade against sin; nor justice in the courthouse to promptly punish crime; nor manhood enough in the nation to put a sheltering arm about innocence and virtue—if it needs lynching to protect woman's dearest possession from the ravening human beasts—then I say lynch, a thousand times a week if necessary."

Opposing the right for Black men to vote was not the only way white suffragists separated themselves from their Black female counterparts. When Mary Ann Shadd Cary, a Black women's suffrage activist, asked leaders of the National American Woman Suffrage Association to place the names of ninety-four Black woman suffragists on their Declaration of the Rights of the Women of the United States, the proposal was denied, historically omitting the work of Black women in the movement. During the first suffrage parade in Washington, DC, in 1913, lead planner Alice Paul instructed Black women to walk at the rear of the march, behind white women. She is the same feminist and women's rights activist who insisted that racial justice and women's justice not be intertwined, her reason being that focusing on obtaining civil rights for Black people would take away from the focus of women earning the right to vote; her ideology defined how white feminism would navigate for decades to come. It separated white feminists from feminists of color, queer feminists, and poor feminists and mirrors the stark differences in outcomes dependent on a woman's identity, then and today.

When the Nineteenth Amendment granted women the right to vote in 1920, very few Black women were able to register to vote after dodging newly enforced laws in the South and West that directly disenfranchised Black Americans. From poll taxes, literacy tests, and grandfather clauses to more dangerous ploys like lynchings and intimidation at the polls, various tactics were implemented to keep Black women and men from casting their ballots. Despite nearly four thousand lynchings of primarily Black men, between 1877 and 1950, for perceived infractions including attempting to register to vote, the efforts of white women's suffrage activists did not increase to combat the discriminatory obstacles and challenges their Black women counterparts faced. It did not matter to them—white women's right to vote had been granted. It wasn't until forty-five years later—and forty-five years of Black women advocating for themselves—that Black women's right to vote was secured through the Voting Rights Act of 1965. However, not much has changed regarding disenfranchisement. Republican legislatures are persistent in passing laws that intend to restrict access to voting in several states, like implementing voter ID requirements. Today, and since the 1800s, Black women have pioneered a movement to make voting a more fair process for everyone, yet we often find ourselves as our only advocates.

Consider the modern-day feminist movement, which has been entirely co-opted by white women and transformed into a mechanism for capitalistic gain. In Koa Beck's *White Feminism*, the author explores the ways in which white feminism became a branded movement that looks very similar to its historical start:

> And much like white feminism practiced by suffragettes, all of these profit-oriented and transactional interactions with politics have produced a "feminist lifestyle"—an aesthetic, a series of slogans, symbols, colors, and shorthands to live on flags or mugs, depending if it's 1920 or 2020, but all available for purchase. Co-working spaces, clubs, conferences, branded experiences—that are very much tied to a Macy's or *Cosmopolitan* magazine or The Wing. Coming to feminism with a centralizing of self was concurrent with the sharp uptick in "women's empowerment," a term that was searched to peak popularity on Google in 2014. Sanitizing "empowerment" away from radical, deeply historic

activism was pivotal for fourth-wave white feminism because it had to become transactional—something you could buy, obtain, and experience as a product rather than an amorphous feeling that rushed in from challenging power.

Not only has white feminism proven to be exclusionary, it also proves time and time again to be self-seeking and one-dimensional. There is a long history of media portraying white women as the only pioneers of change and progressive leaps, while intentionally suppressing a platform for the Black women who played an integral part in these efforts. The 1913 Washington Woman Suffrage Procession was destined for media coverage, so it's no surprise that white suffragettes ordered Black suffragettes to walk at the rear of the parade so that the white suffragettes could be seen. The only Black suffragette captured on camera from that day was journalist Ida B. Wells, who refused to segregate and positioned herself at the front of the line. A notable force in the women's voting rights movement, Wells held a prominent career reporting on lynching, social justice, and organizing on behalf of the movement, yet her white feminist counterparts were only interested in reaping the benefits of her efforts, not highlighting her as the person behind those efforts.

It reminds me of the various times Ugandan activist Vanessa Nakate has been left out of event coverage pertaining to climate change activism, during times when she was quite literally present. The most appalling example was a 2020 photo taken at the World Economic Forum in Davos, Switzerland. The image displayed Nakate, Isabelle Axelsson, Luisa Neubauer, Greta Thunberg, and Loukina Tille, all members of the Fridays for Future movement, but when the Associated Press shared the photo to accompany an article titled "Thunberg Brushes Off Mockery from US Finance Chief," its version of the image was cropped, featuring only the four white activists and removing the only person of color. "I was not on the list of participants. None of my comments from the press conference were included," said the twenty-three-year-old activist in a tweet. "It was like I wasn't even there." It isn't the only time Nakate has been overshadowed by her white climate activist counterparts in the media. She's been left out from several news articles and coverage pertaining to events that she attended, losing the spotlight to Thunberg almost every time, which Thunberg has been persistent in calling out. It shows the ways in which the media and leading corporations are extremely intentional about which women they deem deserving of the spotlight, just as the media intentionally did not photograph Black women in 1913 at the Washington Woman Suffrage Procession; 107 years later, it seems not much has changed.

The Black women I spoke with for this book described white feminism as pseudo activism and felt that it has never been intended for anyone who isn't a white woman. A twenty-seven-year-old Black woman working in corporate diversity, equity, and inclusion in Brooklyn said,

> White feminism is a unique brand of feminism that is riddled with racism, it's feminism reserved for people that look like them. It's very exclusionary and white women don't really subscribe to the causes that women of color have to face, especially Black women. There is kind of an underlying racism from white feminism that is really pervasive. It's conscious, it's unconscious, it's overt, it's covert. And it's really powerful. I feel like Black feminism is the actual core, or the root of, all feminism, because we are the most overlooked, the most underrated, the most persecuted, the most disrespected, etc. So the feminism that we champion and the causes that we care about actually impacts all women. All women benefit and succeed from what we put forth and what we decide to act upon. Black feminism is the best form of feminism because it actually is all encompassing in so many ways, whether that's intentional or not. If we are doing things to improve our circumstances as Black women, it automatically improves circumstances for other women of color and other women in general. So it's the most effective form of feminism.

One thirty-five-year-old Black woman in Berwyn, Pennsylvania, described white feminism as a replacement of white male power: "It's in alignment with a patriarchal power structure that is feminism in name only, but basically you just have white women holding power like white men, or replacing white men."

One thirty-two-year-old Black woman in Dallas, Texas, said, "A lot of Black feminism focuses on community in a way that white feminism does not. In my experience, white feminism has been very individualistic, like 'I myself need these rights in order to do the thing I wanna do.' Meanwhile Black feminism is community-based and focuses on being a leader and a role model in that community and lifting everybody up along with you."

A twenty-seven-year-old Black woman in Austin, Texas, shared,

> I feel like within the workplace, I've definitely experienced the white feminist urge—as the people on Twitter would say—to just talk about how much of an ally they are, and a lot of lip service and just verbally saying they support women of color, peers of color, or people of color. But then if you were to actually look at their actions and really ask about the actionable items that they're doing in this so-called feminist work that they say they do and say is important to them, there isn't really much to back it up. They don't have any women of color in their friend circles, they don't champion, mentor, or sponsor any women of color, they've never directly called out or defended somebody who was offending women of color in the workplace. I feel like that's the most common experience I've had

with white feminism. But I have also had the complete opposite experience and I'm very fortunate for that. I've dealt with white women and white leaders who are my biggest cheerleaders, champions. Who may not always understand some of the issues that I face as a Black woman in corporate America, but they are empathetic and open-minded. It comes down to the individual, but collectively, I don't see this kind of support happening from white women at large.

Feminism, defined as the advocacy of women's rights on the basis of the equality of the sexes, cannot be met without equality of the races, of social statuses, of sexual orientation. This lack of regard seems to be the basis for why white feminism has proven time and time again not to be intersectional or garner impactful change. As many of the Black woman interviewees expressed, white feminism comes off as feminism that focuses on being at the same level as white men, instead of breaking down the patriarchal system that white men created. It doesn't really consider other oppressions aside from financial and gender oppression. Other defining aspects of feminism, like class and immigration status, rarely make the cut.

Historically, this country has always favored white women as more desirable, as needing protection, and as beneficiaries of civil rights more than any other women. While they do fall behind white men in the social hierarchy, they are more privileged than any man of color, and woman of color, in America. They are second—a high place to be. A place that doesn't as often result in organizing, boycotting, mobilizing, and creating mutual aid, because while things might not be the best, they're still pretty damn good. Community is no longer strongly necessary for white women to survive in contemporary America given their perhaps ironic protection within the white male patriarchal order. When my ancestors were outside in scorching weather, being beaten and subjected to extreme labor, white women were inside their house, overseeing someone else preparing their meals, looking after their children, and doing their shopping. When Black suffragists were organizing to obtain a fair voting system, and dodging racism and lynchings, white women were already casting their ballots. When Black women in Georgia began mobilizing Democratic voters to support Biden, saving all women from experiencing four more years of dangerous sexist and misogynist rhetoric from a man who was the subject of multiple accusations of sexual assault and misconduct, 55 percent of white women were out supporting that man, because relatively speaking, things were going to be fine for them.

It was during a Women's Month work seminar that I first realized white feminism was even a thing, and how little it resonated with any of my values, or the values of notable feminists of color before me. Somehow, I had managed to avoid highly publicized conferences with majority-white lineups and dodge the "well behaved women don't make history" coffee mug ads circulating around social media. But I couldn't sit out on this meeting because my manager made attendance mandatory for the people on my team. Introduced as a "girl boss" and "the woman taking the tech industry back from men," a young, blond white woman who had just launched her own startup appeared in the Zoom meeting. I could see the smiles, the inspiration my white women coworkers felt just from being in a seminar with this woman, but I felt whatever she had to say would be a combination of witty phrases, sound advice I could find in an *Elite Daily* article, and quotes from other white businesswomen. And after hearing her speech, I was right. In her background, or what she claimed was how she got her start, each opportunity she listed seemed to happen because of luck. She was lucky enough to attend a reputable four-year university and graduate without any debt (because her parents paid her college tuition), she was lucky enough to land her first job at a top Fortune 500 company because she "networked her ass off" in college, she was lucky enough to go on to graduate school and earn an MBA (which her company at the time paid for), and she was lucky to have people who believed in her and invested in her idea, which led her to starting her own business. The audience seemed impressed and amazed, as if they had never heard a story like this before. To me, it seemed the opposite of impressive; it was expected. Luck is just another means of inherited generational white wealth. If I had the resources, the racial status, the societally accepted phenotype, the parents with money, a job offer from a company who values me enough to pay for my higher education endeavors, I, too, would open a startup. The mention of luck, over and over again, without the mention of white privilege or economical privilege playing an integral part in getting ahead, didn't paint a full picture of how women like her become successful leaders. When it came to the advice portion of the chat, she told the audience to "lean in," "if you want it, go after it, that's what men do," and "you are the decider of your own fate." Those were the Hallmark card quotes that didn't actually advise me on what to do, the same phrases printed on coffee mugs and tote bags that seemed patently obvious. When during the Q and A portion of the event a Black audience member asked how her privilege helped her outcomes, she responded with something along the lines of "I know there are things that maybe I have that not every single other person I know has, but those things haven't changed how hard it is to be heard and valued as a woman in a room full of men." When probed with another question from an Asian audience member about advice for women of color entrepreneurs who are afforded less funding, fewer chances, and less trust than white women, her advice was again to "demand what you want because you know your value." It was then that I realized feminism is oversaturated with whiteness, and that whiteness is not a criterion for advising other women on social issues, or being the face of movements that are meant to be intersectional. Did she really think that Asian women were not already demanding what they want and leaning in? Did she not understand that advocating for yourself when you're a minority often comes with a ton of repercussions in the workplace? She truly felt her privileges were just "things" and that she wasn't "heard" or "valued" as a woman, when her entire career success is a product of people hearing and valuing her. On top of that, this woman had probably just been paid a hefty fee to talk to a group for an hour about her privileged background and her "fortunate" list of opportunities, and to spew phrases found on coffee mugs in the checkout line at T.J. Maxx.

In *White Feminism*, Beck's reflection on her attendance at feminist conferences with entry fees so high that many women of color could not afford to attend mirrored my experience and the way I felt about these money-making seminars. She writes,

> But while fevered attendees were whooping up thin blonde speakers and scribbling down their "style spirit animal" for their name tag...many women of color couldn't have even afforded to walk in the door. Around the time of this initial conference, the median wealth for single Black women and Latinas was $200 and $100, respectively. This means that even the cheapest ticket for attendance would cost all if not half the money they don't otherwise put toward living expenses. You know what the median wealth for white women was? $15,640.

She points out that the spaces dedicated to feminism are as exclusive in their politics as their price points.

> This is how the business of feminism stays middle class and white in practice. How conversations about

optimizing your "career, health, and love life" are reserved for certain women and decidedly not others. The very basic framework of their lives is not considered for entry.

Even more overt than the price tag, though, was the way in which gendered challenges were presented to us. The biggest trademark of the Fun Fearless Life conference, and others like it that I would attend over the years, was the overall assertion that we could overcome any barrier with enough personal strategy. Enough organization. Enough savvy. Enough list-making... This messaging is incredibly enticing because it erases complex systems and casts you as the maker of your own fate. Deeply institutionalized heterosexist, classist, sexist, and ableist impediments are reframed as something you as a feminist mastermind can control for and overcome. This narrative perpetuates the important cornerstone of white feminism that you can prevail over these circumstances through elaborate personal design. Whether it's business, "work-life balance," lifestyle, or romance, "empowerment" is a process of being an optimized individual in the face of gender or racial discrimination, not part of a collective uprising or an assembled body against systems of institutions.

If white women were to take lessons from the women of color who came before them and who are here now, doing the work all around them, feminism could actually become intersectional in real life instead of on a tote bag. I do believe if white women were to focus less on taking power from white men and instead on creating a powerful community of diverse women, we'd see some immediate change. What is a "nasty woman" who continues to adhere to white decency and respectability politics? What is wokeness without making lifestyle changes? What is the point in saying "D&I is top of mind" if you're extending opportunities to, employing, and promoting only white women? For white women who self-identify as feminists, the modern feminist movement might feel segregating to them, as if they do not have a place or are not welcome. But that feeling is a result of non-white women, specifically Black women, feeling that the movement is not intersectional and doesn't include them or prioritize their asks as much as it does the asks of white women. Real solidarity and power is in unity, but unions don't form without a shared goal. Getting closer to a more just world begins with white women, white people, asking Black women, Black people, how they can truly be an ally, and then turning that information into action, not just knowledge. Only then can allyship create substantial change that will benefit not only Black women, but all women, and simultaneously our male counterparts.

CHAPTER 9

The Road to Healing On- and Offline

On the first day of summer, I hosted a dinner with some of my closest friends to celebrate my newly remodeled kitchen. I purposely invited only Black women, because I wanted my friends to feel comfortable talking about healing from generational and racial trauma—experiences very specific to Black women. I hoped that similarity, in race, in gender, in experience, would allow my friends to bring their full selves to the event. Rather than focusing on men we found attractive or gossiping about people we didn't really know, the theme that night, naturally, was self-care. We talked about the power of manifesting our goals, the struggles we were enduring, and the importance of voicing our wants and needs to those we let into our lives. We hyped one another up for our numerous achievements and offered different ways to support one another in our various endeavors. We confided in one another about our shortcomings, our insecurities, and our emotional states, welcoming honest and open dialogue about mental health, a topic that historically has been disregarded in the Black community. Our talks of self-care did not include trivialities like which candle scent makes us feel the most relaxed or what brand of face mask works the best for clearing out pimples. Instead, we shared practices, methods, and tools that we implemented in our lives to counter the effects of systemic racism and trauma, like muting certain words on Twitter, unfollowing accounts that centered Eurocentric beauty, blocking coworkers on social media, and advocating for raises at our respective jobs. But mostly, we laughed. Uncontrollably, contagiously, and at high volume. It was one of the few dinners I had attended where I felt like I and the people around me were allowed to just be, free from judgment, and that signified that we were healing.

The practice of being, existing as yourself, unapologetically, is one that I learned mostly through music from modern Black women artists. It was Ari Lennox's *Shea Butter Baby* album that made me feel proud of the Black feminine customs and rituals I've embedded into my lifestyle, like lathering my body in oils that emit strong scents and tying my hair up at night in satin scarves as I saw my grandmothers and aunts do. And it was Summer Walker's *Over It* album that made me feel that it was okay to demand what I want from the romantic partners I share my time with and to leave situations that no longer serve me. It was Solange's *A Seat at the Table* that validated the frustration I feel as a young Black woman living in a country that pretends to have healed and righted the wrongs of its racist origins. During summer 2019, it was rapper Megan Thee Stallion's *Hot Girl Summer* expression that caused me and my friends to let loose and reclaim our joy, regardless of what obstacles the world threw at us. At the time, what seemed like a simple phrase to describe looking good during the warmest months of the year turned into a movement representing the idea that people, especially Black women, should live their best life without a care for what others think. In a society where Black women face disproportionate burdens, putting ourselves first is a form of protest, or as we like to call it, radical self-care.

Anytime a Black woman decides to put herself first, advocate for her well-being, revoke access, opt out of work, or create, the act is radical. Because, historically, we have been forced into the role of caregivers for white folk and then later obligated to become caregivers for the Black family unit and community in order to survive in a racist climate, it has never been socially acceptable for Black women to practice self-care by putting themselves first. As Audre Lorde stated in her 1988 essay collection *A Burst of Light*, self-care is "an act of political warfare." In a society formed by oppressive systems, Black women actively choosing to prioritize their rest is a form of resistance and radicalism. The same goes for joy and confidence. When the center of beauty is whiteness, and when struggle is denoted for Black women, being confident and exuding joy become radical actions when displayed by Black women. When Simone Biles wore a leotard featuring a goat head made of silver rhinestones, to symbolize being the greatest of all time (GOAT) in gymnastics, during the U.S. Gymnastics

Championships, critics attacked her for being too cocky. In fact, she wore the leotard as a joke aimed at social media critics who ridicule her for... no specific reason at all. The silliness of it is that Simone quite literally does nothing worth criticizing. She is currently the best at her sport, but people feel threatened by seeing a young Black woman perform highly, and higher than her white counterparts, all while being confident in her abilities. The discomfort people feel from this young Black woman's success is what makes her success radical.

Young Black women today are practicing radical self-care through our own personal choices, but also through the online movements we've created that put our narrative back in *our* hands. In a think piece for *BuzzFeed*, writer Niela Orr said, "Hot Girl Summer has become a shorthand for celebrating femme sensibilities and what's possible when people—but mostly women—give no fucks in their pursuit of some self-defined pleasure. It's a movement energized by chicks who couldn't care less (see Exhibit A, Meg's "WTF I Want"); it operates on power that throws caution to the wind." For Black girls and women who are constantly subjected to microaggressions, gaslighting, misogynoir, sexism, and racism, this ideology is not only important, but also essential to surviving the constant and various harms inflicted upon our mental and emotional well-being. In this newfound practice of healing we are creating for ourselves, not only are young Black women giving less agency to the systems and stereotypes that try to hold us back, but we are reclaiming power in prioritizing our mental health by putting out the images we want to see of ourselves simply to normalize our existence in a world that only tries to shrink it.

Before Hot Girl Summer consumed our social media feeds and found itself co-opted by brands galore, several other notable online movements paved the way for Black girls and women to reclaim their expression and joy and, more importantly, to feel good about themselves. These movements help us heal from generational trauma and the ludicrous standards that we are expected to live up to. In these movements we have developed road maps for building community, stress management, and inner peace that create a balanced relationship with ourselves and with society. With Black women as the focus of these movements, not only are we constructing our own narratives, gatekeeping our creations, and forming avenues for rest and healing in a world that rarely supports our well-being; we are letting the world know that we know our worth and cannot be made Black martyrs.

In 2013, Black Girl Magic was popularized by CaShawn Thompson to "celebrate the beauty, power and resilience of Black women." Black Girl Magic is our ability to defy the odds when the world does everything to hold us back and tries to tear us down when we succeed. Through this movement, Black women congratulate each other's accomplishments, directly counteracting the negativity society places on us in real life and online. What once started as a Twitter hashtag quickly transitioned into a campaign, then a reference in Michelle Obama's 2016 Black Girls Rock! Awards speech and now, a way of life. Everyone from Corinne Bailey Rae and Jamila Woods to Janelle Monáe and Solange Knowles have invoked the concept, bringing universal attention to the numerous gifts and talents Black women possess. But Black Girl Magic wasn't the only cultural concept to grow from 2013. Carefree Black Girls, a movement that aims to showcase the "alternative" representations of Black women, was first hashtagged on Twitter by Zeba Blay that same year. In an article for *The Root*, writer Diamond Sharp describes the movement as a concept that Black women "have used to anchor expressions of individuality and whimsy in the face of the heavy stereotypes and painful realities that too often color discussions of their demographic." Think of young Black women posing in flower crowns, burning sage, posting positive affirmations, and flaunting grills. To be a carefree Black girl is to be whoever you want to be, and fully embrace that identity, without caring what others think of your presentation.

My favorite movement, which played an integral role in nurturing my self-confidence and building my self-esteem during college, is the Melanin Movement, a concept carried out by dark-skinned Black women to take back the narrative surrounding their skin tone and fight against colorism. Instagram and Tumblr accounts dedicated to sharing photos of beautiful Black women of darker shades quickly resulted in *melanin* becoming a buzzword, a flex, and a badge of honor. While TV, film, and music videos so often left us out, through this movement, for the first time in our lives, many young dark-skinned women were able to consume an influx of positive and beautiful images that represented us. Another equally important movement for me has been Black Excellence, a concept that highlights Black success despite adverse circumstances, racism and discrimination, and less support and fewer resources than are enjoyed by our white counterparts. When Simone Biles became the gymnast with the most world champion medals (twenty-five) and the most world champion gold medals (nineteen) in a predominantly white sport; when Megan Thee Stallion won Grammys for Best Rap Performance, Best Rap Song, and Best New Artist, all while pursuing a college degree; when Amanda Gorman, at twenty-two years old, read her inauguration poem during the 2020 presidential election; when Michaela Coel became the first Black woman to take home the Emmy Award for Outstanding Writing for a Limited or Anthology Series or Movie, Black women like me were reminded of just how exceedingly excellent it is to achieve something in industries that once prohibited your attendance and still often discriminate against you.

Not only have these movements made stark changes in representation and created a larger discourse around discrimination in professional settings, they've saved many of us from the "sunken place" society has tried to throw us into by connecting us, creating a community for us, and making us realize that our experiences are common within our cohort and our beauty is so immense that it is consistently imitated. While a support group may not be present at our jobs or the work events we attend, we have more access than ever to other Black women's friendships, thoughts, advice, and experiences because of social media, meet-ups, and podcasts. Through these mediums, we've been able to advocate for one another, support one another, and create the most viral and imitated content on social media platforms. Most of these movements involve Black women being large in their expression, as opposed to shrinking ourselves. They ask us to show up fully, as opposed to a watered-down version of ourselves driven by respectability politics and white decency norms. Engaging in these movements not only inspires Black women to unlearn the roles white people have placed on us; it's also provided us an outlet through which to say "fuck you" to the various systems designed to keep us down.

Perhaps we have chosen the online world to infiltrate our movements not only because information spreads fast and communities can be formed quickly, but to reclaim our power in one of the darkest places to be if you're a Black woman. Signing up to be a member of any social media platform means allowing others access to you. Whether it be access from anonymous, racist internet trolls, or exposure to racism through the news cycle or the unsolicited thoughts of others, social media has proven to be an unsafe environment for Black people overall. Black women are constantly reminded of the ways America does not value us as much as other human beings, and are constantly subjected to non-Black women cosplaying in our cultural expression, white brands co-opting our style, and opportunities being awarded to everyone but us, all of which can be extremely toxic to witness. The same movements that were meant for others to respect us and see us often have resulted in others realizing our worth, our beauty, and our innovativeness and eventually capitalizing off it too. From the shape of our lips to the tone of our skin, there's a trend where non-Black women all over the world are trying to achieve our look and receiving accolades, desire, and opportunities because of it, while we remain neglected and considered last. This niche and individual experience that Black women have with social media as a tool subconsciously used by others to imitate and erase us is why we continue to infiltrate our timelines by showcasing, appreciating, and boosting Blackness on Black women—because no one else will. It's our way of saying we belong here too; in fact, we started this shit. It's a way to remind people that we will not be bullied or degraded for our looks and expressions, which so many other people constantly imitate. It's a way to include ourselves in the narratives that society so often sets aside for other women. Ultimately, it's an act of self-care.

We know Blackness is special, and so do all the other groups of people who consciously and unconsciously try to tap into it, but Black women have found some grace in only uplifting what is authentic—and that is the beauty, success, style, and wisdom of other Black women, not non-Black Instagram influencers who try to talk like us or reality TV stars who try to look like us. Some women might view this as segregation, and the opposite of intersectional, while not pausing to notice the erasure that is happening online and in real life for us, as a product of other women playing into it. Oftentimes, we have no control over how we are perceived, because non-Black people control that perception through the way they cosplay in our expression, oftentimes overcompensating and exaggerating, which then negatively affects how we are portrayed. When non-Black celebrities and influencers switch to an exaggerated blaccent for shits and giggles, it doesn't cause the viewer to necessarily perceive non-Black women as uneducated or ghetto. Instead, it supports the stereotype and belief that Black women are uneducated and ghetto, that all Black women talk like this, that Black women cannot be taken seriously. Through their cosplay, not only are these people with influence controlling the narrative of Black women, but they are also contributing to the harmful stereotypes that are used to discredit Black women.

Outside of the online movements young Black women are creating for our representation and well-being, there is a newfound emergence of Black women celebrities publicizing their own struggles with mental health online and in the media. Naomi Osaka, Summer Walker, Doja Cat, and Ari Lennox have all spoken publicly about their battles with anxiety and depression. Their stories shed light on the very real, but highly overlooked, mental health crisis taking the lives of young Black women. In a 2021 article for *Time* titled "Suicide among Black Girls Is a Mental Health Crisis Hiding in Plain Sight," writer Kyra Alessandrini explores the alarming, and underreported, rise in suicide among young Black girls. Highlighting that Black children are two times more likely to die by suicide compared to white children, the piece also explored the various reasons the suicide rate among young Black girls might be rising, online bullying being one of them. The suicide "epidemic" itself has been framed as a largely white issue, especially with respect to rich white kids in pressure cooker high schools, like the media coverage surrounding Palo Alto in 2015. Then there are popular TV shows and films like *13 Reasons Why* and *The Perks of Being a Wallflower*, which reinforce teen suicide as a white bullying issue only, leading society to completely neglect the suicide issues of children of color.

According to a 2020 study published in the *Journal of Applied Developmental Psychology*, Black teenagers face an average of five racially discriminatory experiences every day. Bullying is a leading cause of suicide among school-age children, but bullying toward Black children is often laced with racism. And during the digital age, most of this bullying and racism is happening online. Research proves that girls are more susceptible to mental health issues related to social media use and cyberbullying than boys, and the issue just increases for children of color, who are often subjected to traumatic experiences just from logging on. Videos of Black people being murdered by police, images of lynching, racial slurs, incidents of white privilege that remind Black people of their low place in the social hierarchy, and more are posted so often that they're almost completely unavoidable for these teenagers.

Another leading cause of depression and suicidal thoughts among Black girls and woman is sexual assault. Victims of sexual violence are more prone to experience depression and thoughts of suicide than those who are not victims, and Black girls and women are more likely to be victims of sexual violence than any other girls and women in America. Furthermore, a 2014 Bureau of Justice Statistics study found that 75 percent of victims of sexual assault experience "socioemotional problems," a number that is higher than for almost every other crime. To add to that, a 2020 American Psychological Association study found that Black women and girls "experience significantly higher rates of psychological abuse—including humiliation, insults, name-calling and coercive control—than do women overall." All of this to say that it comes as no surprise that there is an uptick in suicide among Black girls and women. To be exact, 15 percent of Black female high school students attempted suicide leading up to the CDC's 2019 Youth Risk Behavior Survey. When compared to the roughly 9 percent of white female students and 12 percent of Hispanic female students who attempted suicide, the rate becomes more alarming. From 2001 to 2017, the actual suicide death rates for Black American girls ages thirteen to nineteen increased by 182 percent alone, yet it's still unclear whether Black girls are losing their lives to suicide at greater rates than in years before, or if those deaths weren't as accurately reported. Women, adolescents, and people of color are highly underrepresented groups in data, mirroring the reason why the suicide deaths of Black girls have slipped through the cracks in previous years—their intersectional identity itself is rarely accounted for. And then there are the systems that were never put in place to protect Black girls and women. Oftentimes, reports of depression and suicidal thoughts by Black women are undertreated or completely ignored. When twelve-year-old Stormiyah Denson-Jackson, who died from suicide in 2018, reported being bullied to her teachers and administrators, no one listened. The same neglect happened to ten-year-old Isabella Tichenor, who reported being bullied for being Black and autistic to her teachers, the school administration, and the district administration. According to a news report covering the tragedy, "a federal investigation of the Davis School District found a pattern of ignoring complaints of racial harassment." It reflects the lack of care and increased gaslighting Black girls and women face in general when seeking support or expressing their troubles.

While experts conclude that with regular social, emotional, and psychological support, suicide can be avoided, the formula is not as simple for Black girls and women. Instead, researchers also suggest teaching young Black girls coping skills like resilience and emotional regulation to equip them with the tools required to understand, vocalize, and manage their feelings. But it shouldn't fall on young Black girls to be resilient and regulate their emotions during times of adversity that other children are not expected to deal with and do not encounter to the same degree. It is not the responsibility of Black girls and women to brush off and ignore the discrimination and harm inflicted upon them for their entire lifetime.

Instead of expecting Black girls and women to adjust, society needs to shift.

Luisa Bonifacio, a New York–based psychologist, believes the depression and suicidal thoughts of Black women cannot be tied to one or two causes, but instead to multilayered oppressions, which makes the solution more complex than ignoring and brushing off these causes:

> What I'm seeing and most connecting to the increase in depression and suicides is a lot of isolation. In a lot of ways it's feeling isolated socially, just not feeling supported or seen, or understood culturally, and kind of feeling left out. I think the experience of Black women is so diverse and so unique, but I think for a lot of Black women, who are struggling with depression and suicidal thoughts, is a real intense feeling of no one understanding them or that they don't belong. We see that systemic oppression is real, racism is real, and misogyny is real. And so I think Black women usually are bearing the brunt of all those systems.

To combat these issues that young Black women endure, therapy is the most obvious method for healing, but oftentimes Black women face heightened challenges when seeking support. Given that Black therapists account for just 4 percent of psychologists, it becomes difficult for Black women to locate a therapist who understands their lived experiences and cultural perspective, and then also has availability and accepts their insurance. While seeing a therapist of the same racial background is not everyone's be-all and end-all, it's important to work with someone who holds knowledge and experience about the impacts of systemic racism and misogynoir on Black women in order for sessions to be productive and effective. And while mental health in the Black community is slowly being destigmatized, Black women are more likely to take on primary caregiving for their children, work long hours, and juggle multiple projects at once (like hold a job while taking classes or have a side gig on top of full-time employment), meaning they often face greater demands on their time. More impactfully, the pressure to appear strong and unbothered while managing different demands, as a result of being socialized to be strong and resilient, makes it unclear to some young Black women that they're actually in need of support. Couple these barriers with the cost of the therapy and it is not exactly shocking to learn that many young Black women are not seeing a therapist.

Optimistically, Bonifacio has noted a dramatic increase in young Black women seeking support in other ways, especially since the summer of 2020, when social media accounts dedicated to Black mental health and Black therapy gained popularity as a response to the various traumatic experiences unfolding for the Black community. The national phenomenon has pushed the conversation forward and pushed people to embrace it more by joining mental health groups and summits, taking part in group conversations, and following self-care professionals online to absorb their recommendations and teachings. Even Black celebrities like Simone Biles and Naomi Osaka have been holding public conversations surrounding mental health, having a huge impact on normalizing and prioritizing the well-being of Black women. Additionally, Black women have established a bond with others in our own community, whether online or through meet-up groups, from shared experiences, conditions, and understanding, which often is great enough to combat the negative effects of our traumas. A 2010 study published in the *Social Service Review* found that social support has positive effects on someone's well-being, speaking to the importance of community identity among Black women. When we view our racial and ethnic identities as positive, despite the world feeding us and everyone else the opposite image, we are more likely to have higher self-esteem, more confidence, and better overall mental health. That's why Black women who publicly bask in their Blackness and uplift other Black women, like Serena Williams, Beyoncé, Solange, Janelle Monáe, Megan Thee Stallion, Lizzo, Issa Rae, Michaela Coel, Zendaya, Simone Biles, and so many more are so important to our positive movements. It's why Netflix's "Hey Queen" videos and Instagram accounts like @blackgirlmagicfeed and @melanin.feed are so important. These prominent figures in pop culture and forms of affirming media remind us of our beauty when so many other public figures and forms of media try to co-opt our beauty or deploy it. They remind us, and the world, that there is nothing wrong with being unapologetically Black, carefree, happy, and confident. They uplift Black women, Blackness, and Black womanhood to the masses, the same way we do on the ground, within our cohorts.

For Black women, self-care goes beyond physical fitness or consumerism, like buying into massage subscriptions or purchasing high-end skincare products. In most cases, it is what media we allow ourselves to consume, what conversations we allow ourselves to be a part of, and who we allow ourselves to be around. And until the world begins to give us respect and show up for us the way we have so often shown up for everyone else, it should be rightfully understood why we are protective of our space and whom we allow into it. For many of the Black women I spoke with, self-care has taken the form of revoking access. From leaving jobs that have a toxic environment, to blocking individuals on Instagram who inflict harm upon them, many young Black women are taking care of themselves through cutting people off. Others are going to therapy, joining community groups, and prioritizing their friendships. Some are raising their standards for their employer, significant other, friends, and family. Many of us are calling out our older family members about internalized racism and problematic practices that created childhood trauma for us, like "tough love," respectability politics, being told not to cry, and beatings. By actively deciding to put our wellness before anyone or anything else, our self-care becomes a form of protest against a society that is determined to oppress us to a breaking point and is essential in a world that does not allow space for Black women to grieve, express frustration, or receive support.

As society continues to provide us with few options in making conditions better for ourselves, penalizes us for being opposed to these unfair conditions, and expects us to remain calm, kind, and respectable when given the worst of the pick, young Black women are expressing their rage through solidarity with one another, highlighting their worth to the masses through social media, protecting their peace, and advocating for more or choosing to walk away if those needs are not met. From the moment we are born, our environment begins teaching us that we are different from our peers. We aren't afforded innocence in our childhood, we aren't allowed to make mistakes, we aren't perceived as human. During youth, we are ridiculed for the things we cannot change and for our cultural presentation, yet as we grow older, we witness other people copy and profit off these same characteristics. Then, if our skin is dark, if our hair is nappy, if our nose is too wide, we face ridicule again, from our peers and from total strangers online, again, about something we cannot change. So, we learn to soften our Blackness, not because we want to, but because we've witnessed the ways palatability can sometimes lead to opportunity, support, and being treated with decency. But as we mature, and grow wiser in our relationships, it becomes apparent to many of us that palatability is a false ideology and that it doesn't really change our conditions at all, because racism is much more complex than assimilating and code-switching, or fitting a standard. On top of these various setbacks and traumatic experiences, we're faced with micro-aggressions in the workplace, racism online, policing at the store, discrimination in medical settings, virtue signaling from our white peers, and an unrealistic expectation to always display strength and satisfaction. But we aren't satisfied. Not at all. And collectively, I think we've realized that and are becoming okay with letting others know we are not okay. That things are not okay. That the way we are treated is not okay. That what is expected of us is not okay. And even though the world still seems to not be completely receptive, we are exercising ways to take care of ourselves. This might look like our circles getting Blacker and less racially diverse the older we get, or choosing not to engage in non-work-related chatter with the white women at our jobs. It could even mean only dating within our race, not because we don't find non-Black people attractive, but because the energy and time that often goes into getting someone to understand our position is not always worth it. It might look like twerking on Instagram Live to show how we display our joy despite the adversity in the world, or it could be quitting a job, a friendship, a romantic relationship that is not serving us nearly as much as we are serving others. Maybe it's flexing how the sun makes our skin glisten in an Instagram photo or going on a Twitter rant about microaggressions so others can know our experiences are real. Perhaps it's a radical action, like prioritizing rest in a world that expects Black women to always be available to others. Whatever it looks like, Black women are valid in how they choose to grant themselves grace until others begin granting us grace and take a walk in our shoes.

ACKNOWLEDGMENTS

There are many people to thank for helping me with this book. First, the numerous Black women who allowed me to hear and share their stories, showing me that strength and vulnerability can actually be synonymous. Abena and Leah, who were the first people to read *In Our Shoes*, and reviewed and provided suggestions for every chapter. Amber, my editor, who fully understood the vision and need for this project. Sarah, my agent, who helped me settle on this idea and believed in my strengths as a writer. Heather, my dear friend and former editor, who reviewed the proposal for this book. Chioma, for being the first person to tell me I should write a book. My support circle of close friends, who consistently recognized the time and energy I put into this project and always offered to be a listening ear. And lastly, my parents, who did their best to raise a headstrong, confident daughter because they knew the world would be nothing like the fairy-tale books I grew up reading.

NOTES

Chapter 1: It's Different in My Body

8 **Nearly 34 percent of missing girls:** "2020 NCIC Missing Persons and Unidentified Person Statistics," FBI, https://www .fbi.gov/file-repository/2020-ncic-missing-person-and -unidentified-person-statistics.pdf/view.

19 ***Politico* interview with Senator Bill Cassidy:** "View from the Hill: A Conversation with Sen. Bill Cassidy," Harvard T. H. Chan School of Public Health, premiered May 19, 2022, YouTube video, 28:09, https://www.youtube.com/watch?v=pyqAO2CGb74.

21 **University of Virginia's Seanna Leath:** Seanna Leath, Martinque K. Jones, and Sheretta Butler-Barnes, "An Examination of ACEs, the Internalization of the Superwoman Schema, and Mental Health Outcomes among Black Adult Women," *Journal of Trauma and Dissociation* 23, no. 3 (May–June 2022): 307–323, https://pubmed.ncbi.nlm.nih.gov /34622746/.

22 **Additionally, a 2016 study:** Kelly M. Hoffman, Sophie Trawalter, Jordan R. Axt, and M. Norman Oliver, "Racial Bias in Pain Assessment and Treatment Recommendations, and False Beliefs about Biological Differences between Blacks and Whites," *Proceedings of the National Academy of Sciences of the United States of America* 113, no. 16 (April 4, 2016): 4296–4301, https:// www.pnas.org/doi/10.1073/pnas.1516047113.

22 **According to the American Bar Association:** Kiara M. Bridges, "Implicit Bias and Racial Disparities in Health Care," American Bar Association, https://www.americanbar.org /groups/crsj/publications/human_rights_magazine_home /the-state-of-healthcare-in-the-united-states/racial-disparities -in-health-care/.

22 **a study observing four hundred hospitals:** Bridges, "Implicit."

32 **video of a Rochester police officer:** Nicole Hong, "Rochester Officers Suspended after Pepper-Spraying of 9-Year-Old Girl," *New York Times*, January 31, 2021, https://www.nytimes.com/2021/01 /31/nyregion/rochester-police-pepper-spray-child.html.

32 **A 2019 Georgetown Law study:** Jamilia J. Blake and Rebecca Epstein, "Listening to Black Women and Girls: Lived Experiences of Adultification Bias," Georgetown Law Center on Poverty and Inequality, https://www.law.georgetown.edu/poverty-inequality -center/wp-content/uploads/sites/14/2019/05/Listening-to -Black-Women-and-Girls.pdf.

33 **A 2017 study conducted:** Jamilia J. Blake, Rebecca Epstein, and Thalia González, "Girlhood Interrupted: The Erasure of Black Girls' Childhood," Georgetown Law Center on Poverty and Inequality, June 27, 2017, https://ssrn.com/abstract=3000695.

37 **study called "Gender and Trauma":** Rebecca Epstein and Thalia González, "Gender and Trauma: Somatic Interventions for Girls in Juvenile Justice: Implications for Policy and Practice," Georgetown Law Center on Poverty and Inequality, April 25, 2017, https://ssrn.com/abstract=2965674.

Chapter 2: Leave the Box Braids for the Black Girls

55 **Union told ESPN:** Katie Barnes, "'Bring It On': From Spirit Fingers to Appropriation, the Cult Sports Film Is Much More

than a Teen Rom-Com," ESPN, August 25, 2020, https://www
.espn.com/espn/story/_/id/29731506/bring-spirit-fingers
-appropriation-cult-sports-film-much-more-teen-rom-com.

55 **Anna P. Kambhampaty:** Anna P. Kambhampaty, "The A.S.L.
Interpretation of 'WAP' Was TikTok Gold. It's Also a Problem,"
New York Times, August 14, 2021, https://www.nytimes.com
/2021/08/14/style/asl-wap-tiktok.html.

55 **"WAP" into an ASL dance:** Raven Sutton, "WAP—Cardi B ft.
Megan Thee Stallion (ASL)," YouTube video, 2021, https://www
.youtube.com/shorts/alVTEH-Yviw.

55 **They are signing songs:** Kambhampaty, "The A.S.L.
Interpretation of 'WAP' Was TikTok Gold."

57 *Bustle* **profiled Addison Rae:** Carrie Batan, "The Millennials'
Guide to Addison Rae," *Bustle*, April 14, 2021, https://www
.bustle.com/entertainment/addison-rae-interview-acting-politics.

60 **When Gwen Stefani released:** Bianca Gracie, "Gwen Stefani's
'Love. Angel. Music. Baby.' Turns 15: A Track-by-Track
Retrospective with the Pop Superstar," *Billboard*, November 11,
2019, https://www.billboard.com/music/pop/gwen-stefani
-interview-love-angel-music-baby-15th-anniversary-8543814/.

63 **In her essay "Racial Plagiarism":** Minh-Ha T. Pham, "Racial
Plagiarism and Fashion," *QED: A Journal in GLBTQ
Worldmaking* 4, no. 3 (Fall 2017): 67–80, https://www.jstor.org
/stable/10.14321/qed.4.3.0067

63 **hair stylist Guido Palau:** Rob Moran, "Marc Jacobs Called Out
for Putting Dreadlocks on Models at New York Fashion Week,"
The Sydney Morning Herald, September 16, 2016, https://www
.smh.com.au/lifestyle/fashion/marc-jacobs-called-out-for
-putting-dreadlocks-on-models-at-new-york-fashion-week
-20160916-grhklt.html.

64 **As Pham puts it:** Jonathan Square, "Is Instagram's Newest
Sensation Just Another Example of Cultural Appropriation?,"

Fashionista, March 27, 2018, https://fashionista.com/2018/03
/computer-generated-models-cultural-appropriation.

64 **titled "What Is Digital Blackface?":** Madeline Howard,
"What Is Digital Blackface? Experts Explain Why the Social
Media Practice Is Problematic," *Women's Health*, February 11,
2022, https://www.womenshealthmag.com/life/a33278412
/digital-blackface/.

65 **"too much 'Lamborghini'":** Rania Aniftos, "Miley Cyrus
Apologizes for Controversial 2017 Hip-Hop Comments: 'Simply
Said, I F-ed Up,'" *Billboard*, https://www.billboard.com/music
/music-news/miley-cyrus-apologizes-hip-hop-comments
-2017-8515574/.

67 **article for *Paper* magazine:** Wanna Thompson, "How White
Women on Instagram Are Profiting Off Black Women," *Paper*,
November 14, 2018, https://www.papermag.com/white-women
-blackfishing-instagram-2619714094.html?rebelltitem
=13#rebelltitem13.

Chapter 3: Why Are You So Dark?

74 **unfair disciplinary action:** Sarah Webb, "Recognizing and
Addressing Colorism in Schools," *Learning for Justice*, January
25, 2016, https://www.learningforjustice.org/magazine
/recognizing-and-addressing-colorism-in-schools.

74 **lower socioeconomic status:** Latocia Keyes, Eusebius Small,
and Silviya Nikolova, "The Complex Relationship between
Colorism and Poor Health Outcomes with African Americans: A
Systematic Review," *Analyses of Social Issues and Public Policy*
20 (November 26, 2020): 676–697, https://spssi.onlinelibrary
.wiley.com/doi/10.1111/asap.12223?af=R.

74 **more vulnerable to incarceration:** Makala Desargent,
"Colorism within the Black Community and Health Disparities,"

Scaffold 3 (Spring 2021), https://ejournals.library.vanderbilt.edu
/index.php/UWS/article/view/5114/2871.

74 **dark-skinned Black women receive sentences:** Jandel
Crutchfield and Amy Fisher, "Colorism and Police Killings,"
Western Journal of Black Studies 41, nos. 3–4 (December 2017):
81–91, https://www.researchgate.net/publication/330689074
_Colorism_and_Police_Killings.

75 **drawn from the National Health Interview Survey:** US
Department of Health and Human Services, National Center for
Health Statistics, "National Health Interview Survey, 2005,"
Inter-University Consortium for Political and Social Research
(December 21, 2006), https://www.icpsr.umich.edu/web/NACDA
/studies/4606/publications.

75 **National Survey of American Life:** James S. Jackson et al.,
"The National Survey of American Life: A Study of Racial,
Ethnic, and Cultural Influences on Mental Disorders and Mental
Health," *International Journal of Methods in Psychiatric
Research* 13, no. 4 (2004), https://scholar.harvard.edu/files
/davidrwilliams/files/2004-the_national_survey-williams.pdf.

80 **ten-step checklist:** Sarah Webb (@colorismhealing), "10
Warning Signs You Have Colorist Friends," Instagram photo,
September 17, 2021, https://www.instagram.com/p/CT7I
-XMgnQr/.

82 **A 2013 study exploring:** Gene H. Brody et al., "Exploring the
Impact of Skin Tone on Family Dynamics and Race-Related
Outcomes," *Journal of Family Psychology* 27, no. 5 (2013):
817–826, https://www.ncbi.nlm.nih.gov/pmc/articles
/PMC3970169/.

82 **parents of dark-skinned children:** Nancy Boyd-Franklin,
"Racism, Racial Identity, and Skin Color Issues," in *Black Families
in Therapy*, 2nd ed. (New York: Guilford Publications, 2003),
28–51, https://www.guilford.com/excerpts/boydfranklin2.pdf?t.

82 **while other parents may provide:** Beverly A. Greene, "Sturdy Bridges: The Role of African-American Mothers in the Socialization of African-American Children," *Women and Therapy* 10, nos. 1–2 (September 11, 2009): 205–225, https://www.tandfonline.com/doi/abs/10.1300/J015v10n01_18.

83 **I asked Mena to tell me:** All "Mena" quotes in this chapter are sourced from a phone interview conducted by the author in September 2021.

86 **small Catholic high school:** Phone interview conducted with the author in September 2021.

90 **"Alongside black boys and men":** Tobi Kyeremateng, "How Colourism and Misogynoir Affected a Generation of Dark-Skinned Black Women On and Off the Timeline," *Gal-Dem*, May 1, 2020, https://gal-dem.com/how-colourism-and-misogynoir-affected-a-generation-of-dark-skinned-black-women-twitter/.

91 **episode of *Dark Girls 2*:** "How Social Media Has Helped Black Women Reclaim Their Beauty," episode in *Dark Girls 2*, written and directed by D. Channsin Berry, aired June 24, 2020, on OWN, https://www.oprah.com/own-darkgirls2/how-social-media-has-helped-black-women-reclaim-their-beauty.

Chapter 4: The Not-So-Token Black Friend

110 **research on code-switching:** Courtney L. McCluney et al., "The Costs of Code-Switching," *Harvard Business Review*, November 15, 2019, https://hbr.org/2019/11/the-costs-of-codeswitching.

114 **"It doesn't matter if you're":** This tweet has been modified for readability in the text. MizFit KiKi (@MizFitKiKi), "It doesn't matter if intro or extra there's ways a reason," Twitter, January 15, 2021, https://twitter.com/MizFitKiKi/status/1350003679315824640?s=20.

115 **"Black women aren't allowed to":** This tweet has been modified for readability in the text. S. LaMartine (@the_SLaMartine), "Black women aren't allowed to be [insert any adjective in dictionary]," Twitter, January 14, 2021, https://twitter.com/the_SLaMartine/status /1349896767811297285?s=20.

115 **"The issue is that there's":** This tweet has been modified for readability in the text. Keshi (@KeshisCutties), "I'm extrovert & I get tired. The issue is that there's usually only one of us in the space," Twitter, January 15, 2021, https://twitter.com /KeshisCuties/status/1350141274607771648?s=20.

115 **"This gets to the heart":** This tweet has been modified for readability in the text. EcoFemMama (@fem_eco), "This gets to the heart of why racial problems persist. I bet most," Twitter, January 14, 2021, https://twitter.com/fem_eco/status /1349905079172739074?s=20.

117 **According to *Harvard Business Review*:** McCluney, "Code-Switching."

Chapter 5: Policing without a Badge

135–136 **By definition, tone policing:** "Tone Policing," Dictionary.com, https://www.dictionary.com/browse/tone-policing#:~:text =noun,an%20argument%20through%20tone%20policing.

144 ***New York Post* called the outburst:** Brian Lewis, "Serena Has Mother of All Meltdowns in US Open Final Loss," *New York Post*, September 8, 2018, https://nypost.com/2018/09/08/serena -has-mother-of-all-meltdowns-in-us-open-final-loss/.

144 **In a *Sportscasting* article:** Jess Bolluyt, "Serena Williams and Other Tennis Players Who Had the Worst Meltdowns," *Sportscasting*, September 9, 2018, https://www.sportscasting .com/worst-meltdowns-in-tennis.

Chapter 6: Burnt the Hell Out

148 **While millennials are the target group:** Nancy Beauregard et al., "Gendered Pathways to Burnout: Results from the SALVEO Study," *Annals of Work Exposures and Health* 62, no. 4 (May 2018): 426–437, https://academic.oup.com/annweh/article/62/4/426/4870017.

148–149 **"accelerated biological aging":** Arline T. Geronimus et al., "Do US Black Women Experience Stress-Related Accelerated Biological Aging?," *Human Nature* 21, no. 1 (March 10, 2021): 19–38, https://www.ncbi.nlm.nih.gov/pmc/articles/PMC2861506/.

149 **"When we're talking about burnout":** All quoted material from Kenya Crawford in this chapter comes from a phone interview conducted by the author in October 2021.

151 **the *Journal of Black Psychology*:** Ijeoma J. Madubata et al., "Helplessness Mediates Racial Discrimination and Depression for African-American Young Adults," *Journal of Black Psychology* 44, no. 7 (2018): 628–643, https://journals.sagepub.com/doi/pdf/10.1177/0095798418811476.

156 **Erin Overbey, a former archive editor:** Erin Overbey (@ErinOverbey), "Let's talk about racism! Most white people at prestigious magazines don't ever want to talk about race or diversity at all," Twitter, September 14, 2021, https://twitter.com/erinoverbey/status/1437767832159277058?s=20.

157 **A spreadsheet was later created:** "#PUBLISHINGPAIDME," GoogleForms, https://docs.google.com/spreadsheets/d/1Xsx6rKJtafa8f_prlYYD3zRxaXYVDaPXbasvt_iA2vA/edit#gid=1798364047.

159 **Black women in America make:** "Black Women and the Pay Gap," AAUW, https://www.aauw.org/resources/article/black-women-and-the-pay-gap/.

159 **are the highest unemployed group:** Thomas Franck and Nate Rattner, "Black and Hispanic Women Aren't Sharing in the Job Market Recovery," CNBC, March 5, 2021, https://www.cnbc.com /2021/03/05/black-and-hispanic-women-arent-sharing-in-the -job-market-recovery.html.

159 **less likely to receive promotions:** Leslie Hunter-Gadsden, "Report: Black Women Less Likely to Be Promoted, Supported by Their Managers," PBS, November 17, 2018, https://www.pbs.org /newshour/economy/report-black-women-less-likely-to-be -promoted-supported-by-their-managers.

159 **According to a 2016 study:** Eileen Patten, "Racial, Gender Wage Gaps Persist in U.S. Despite Some Progress," Pew Research Center, July 1, 2016, https://www.pewresearch.org/fact-tank /2016/07/01/racial-gender-wage-gaps-persist-in-u-s-despite -some-progress/.

159 **height of the COVID-19 pandemic:** Tim Smart, "COVID-19 Job Market Wreaks Havoc on Black Women," *US News & World Report*, April 15, 2021, https://www.usnews.com/news/economy /articles/2021-04-15/black-women-suffering-the-most-from -covid-19-job-market-disruption.

160 **When filmmaker Nikyatu Jusu:** Nikyatu Jusu (@NotNikyatu), "Rarely do I meet Black women who are mediocre or even average in the professional spaces I navigate," Twitter, September 10, 2021, https://twitter.com/NotNikyatu/status /1436401562612535307?s=20.

162 **"I've seen some Black women":** All quotes in this chapter from Mary Balingit come from a phone interview with the author conducted in October 2021.

173 **"When I go to an art gallery":** All quotes in this chapter from Naj Austin come from a phone interview with the author conducted in October 2021.

183 **When Issa Rae revealed:** Jamal Jordan, "Issa Ray and the New Rules of Black TV," *Mic*, https://www.mic.com/culture/issa-rae -cover-story-october-2021.

185 **unwritten rules of Black TV:** Hannah Giorgis, "Not Enough Has Changed Since *Sanford and Son*," *The Atlantic*, September 13, 2021, https://www.theatlantic.com/magazine/archive/2021 /10/the-unwritten-rules-of-black-tv/619816/.

Chapter 7: I Met God, She's Black

191 **poke fun at sacred cows:** Carol Kuruvilla, "Jewish Atheist's Controversial T-Shirt: 'I Met God, She's Black,'" *HuffPost*, January 3, 2015, https://www.huffpost.com/entry/i-met-god -shes-black_n_6406928.

192 **When Jorge Guajardo:** Jorge Guajardo (@jorge_guajardo), "Black women will save the United States," Twitter, August 17, 2020, https://twitter.com/jorge_guajardo/status/1295556 454473256961?s=20.

192 **With sexual assault allegations:** Julia Craven, "5 Black Women Open Up about Being in Violent Relationships," *HuffPost*, April 14, 2017, https://www.huffpost.com/entry /domestic-violence_n_58f0c16ee4b0da2ff85fdd27.

192 **Black women are the fastest-growing:** Valentina Zarya, "This Is Why Women Are the Fastest Growing Prison Population," *Fortune*, December 10, 2015, https://fortune.com/2015/12/10 /prison-reform-women/.

192 **a harder time finding housing:** Julia Craven, "Black Women with Criminal Records Have a Harder Time Than Their White Peers Finding Housing in D.C.," *HuffPost*, October 18, 2016, https://www.huffpost.com/entry/black-white-women-housing -dc_n_5806958fe4b0dd54ce361ad3?ncid=engmodushpmg 00000004.

193 **make up only 3.6 percent:** "Black Women in American Politics: 2017 Status Update," Center for American Women and Politics, https://cawp.rutgers.edu/sites/default/files/resources /bw_2017_status_update.pdf.

195 **As Taylor Crumpton:** Taylor Crumpton, "Black Women Saved the Democrats. Don't Make Us Do It Again," *Washington Post*, November 7, 2020, https://www.washingtonpost.com/outlook /2020/11/07/black-women-joe-biden-vote/.

195 **Ashley Nkadi argued:** Ashley Nkadi, "Y'all Don't Deserve Black Women," *The Root*, December 13, 2017, https://www.theroot.com /yall-dont-deserve-black-women-1821255162.

196 *HuffPost* **writer Julia Craven:** Julia Craven, "Black Women Are a Political Organizing Force. They're Not Unicorns," *HuffPost*, December 13, 2017, https://www.huffpost.com/entry /black-women-doug-jones_n_5a318dede4b091ca268508c2.

196 **A description on tvtropes.org:** "Magical Negro," TV Tropes, https://tvtropes.org/pmwiki/pmwiki.php/Main/MagicalNegro.

197 **Talesha Wilson, a Black feminist:** Talesha Wilson (@SignMyBeauty), "Too often, Black women get the short end of the sticks," Twitter, November 19, 2021, https://twitter.com/Sign MyBeauty_/status/1461701757126561804?s=20&t=lC7IXR 3vfcqa_qzsH8Ftyg.

201 **It results in Black people:** Kelly M. Hoffman, "Racial Bias in Pain Assessment and Treatment Recommendations, and False Beliefs about Biological Differences between Blacks and Whites," *Psychological and Cognitive Sciences* 113, no. 16 (April 4, 2016): 4296–4301, https://www.pnas.org/doi/abs/10.1073/pnas .1516047113.

201 **Black hospital patients:** Todd H. Knox et al., "Ethnicity and Analgesic Practice," *Annals of Emergency Medicine* 35, no. 1 (January 2000): 11–16, https://www.sciencedirect.com/science /article/abs/pii/S0196064400700990.

201 **"A Superhumanization Bias":** Adam Waytz, Kellie Marie Hoffman, and Sophie Trawalter, "A Superhumanization Bias in Whites' Perceptions of Blacks," *Social Psychological and Personality Science*, https://journals.sagepub.com/doi/abs/10.1177/1948550614553642.

201 **Although Black women account:** Sommer Brugal, Marisa Iati, and Jennifer Jenkins, "Nearly 250 Women Have Been Fatally Shot by Police Since 2015," *Washington Post*, https://www.washingtonpost.com/graphics/2020/investigations/police-shootings-women/.

201 **Dajerria Becton was just:** Carol Cole-Frowe and Richard Fausset, "Jarring Image of Police's Use of Force at Texas Pool Party," *New York Times*, June 8, 2015, https://www.nytimes.com/2015/06/09/us/mckinney-tex-pool-party-dispute-leads-to-police-officer-suspension.html.

201 **Breonna Taylor was only twenty-six:** Richard A. Oppel Jr., Derrick Bryson Taylor, and Nicholas Bogel-Burroughs, "What to Know About Breonna Taylor's Death," *New York Times*, August 23, 2022, https://www.nytimes.com/article/breonna-taylor-police.html.

203 **"a subtler form of":** Waytz, Hoffman, and Trawalter, "Superhumanization."

203 **A 2012 study conducted:** Arlene Eisen, *Operation Ghetto Storm* (Malcolm X Grassroots Committee, 2014), https://www.operation ghettostorm.org/uploads/1/9/1/1/19110795/new_all_14_11_04.pdf.

206 **"I dream of never":** Zandashé L'orelia Brown (@zandashe), "I dream of never being called resilient in my life again," Twitter, May 18, 2021, https://twitter.com/zandashe/status/1394805726825099279?s=20.

206 **"I taught mostly Black kids":** Bronwyn Harris (@BronwynAnn), "I taught mostly Black kids in Oakland and people always talked about how resilient they were," Twitter, May

19, 2021, https://twitter.com/BronwynAnn/status/1395204004 385153026?s=20.

206 **"Something has always bothered me":** Arika P. (@arimopat), Twitter, May 21, 2021, https://twitter.com/arimopat/status /1395754103523840007?s=20.

207 **When my friend Maxine posted:** Maxine Simone, "Normalize Weak Black Women," YouTube, December 9, 2021, https://www .youtube.com/watch?v=-SPKLfJCZWk&feature=youtu.be.

208 **2010 study titled "Superwoman Schema":** Cheryl L. Woods-Giscombé, "Superwoman Schema: African American Women's Views on Stress, Strength, and Health," *Qualitative Health Research* 20, no. 5 (February 12, 2010): 668–683, https://www .ncbi.nlm.nih.gov/pmc/articles/PMC3072704/.

208 **According to Arline T. Geronimus:** Arline T. Geronimus et al., "'Weathering' and Age Patterns of Allostatic Load Scores among Blacks and Whites in the Unites States," *American Journal of Public Health* 96, no. 5 (May, 2006): 826–833, https:// www.ncbi.nlm.nih.gov/pmc/articles/PMC1470581/.

209 **neuroendocrinologist Bruce Sherman McEwen and coauthor Huda Akil:** Bruce S. McEwen and Huda Akil, "Revisiting the Stress Concept: Implications for Affective Disorders," *The Journal of Neuroscience* 40, no. 1 (January 2, 2020): 12–21, https://www.jneurosci.org/content/40/1/12.

210 **As R. E. Romero so eloquently:** R. E. Romero, "The Icon of the Strong Black Woman: The Paradox of Strength," in *Psychotherapy with African American Women: Innovations in Psychodynamic Perspective and Practice,* ed. L. C. Jackson and B. Greene (New York: The Guildford Press, 2000), 225–238.

218 **Black women are embracing therapy:** Therapy for Black Girls, https://therapyforblackgirls.com/.

219 **As writer Evie Muir penned:** Evie Muir, "What Is a 'Soft Black Girl Summer'? And Why I'm Vowing to Have One," *Refinery29,*

May 11, 2022, https://www.refinery29.com/en-us/2022/05
/10974812/what-does-soft-black-girl-summer-mean-tiktok.

Chapter 8: Woke

221 **journalist Leslie Streeter tweeted:** Leslie Streeter
(@LeslieStreeter), "'Woke' was a term developed within the
African-American community as a reminder to be aware and
prepared," Twitter, September 13, 2021, https://twitter.com
/LeslieStreeter/status/1437508187792490503?s=20.

223 **Trump had maintained:** Brianna Holt, "White Clicktivism:
Why Are Some Americans Woke Online but Not in Real Life?,"
The Guardian, December 9, 2020, https://www.theguardian
.com/world/2020/dec/09/white-liberals-social-media-activism.

224 **Kayla Wiltfong explores the dissociation:** Kayla Wiltfong,
"Dear White Women, Our Kindness Is Worthless," *UMKS ROO
News*, November 9, 2020, https://kcroonews.com/dear-white
-women-our-kindness-is-worthless/.

225 **35 percent of Biden voters:** Amina Dunn, "Few Trump or
Biden Supporters Have Close Friends Who Back the Opposing
Candidate," Pew Research Center, September 18, 2020, https://
www.pewresearch.org/fact-tank/2020/09/18/few-trump
-or-biden-supporters-have-close-friends-who-back-the
-opposing-candidate/.

227 **Imani Barbarin, a disabled activist:** Imani Barbarin
(@crutches_and_spice), TikTok, June 9, 2021, https://www
.tiktok.com/@crutches_and_spice/video/6971796171522084102.

229 **In a 2015 article for *The Atlantic*:** Ta Nehisi Coates, "There Is
No Post-Racial America, *The Atlantic*, July/August 2015, https://
www.theatlantic.com/magazine/archive/2015/07/post-racial
-society-distant-dream/395255/.

230 **I interviewed Gwen Kansen:** Holt, "White Clicktivism."

234 **Black women are twelve times:** "Giving Birth in America," Every Mother Counts, https://everymothercounts.org/giving -birth-in-america/.

239 **Republican legislatures are persistent:** "Voting Laws Roundup 2017," Brennan Center for Justice, May 10, 2017, https:// www.brennancenter.org/our-work/research-reports/voting -laws-roundup-2017.

239 **"feminism practiced by suffragettes":** Koa Beck, *White Feminism: From the Suffragettes to Influencers and Who They Leave Behind* (New York: Simon & Schuster, 2021), 104.

248 **"But while fevered attendees":** Beck, *White Feminism*, 105.

248 **"the business of feminism":** Beck, *White Feminism*, 105–106.

Chapter 9: The Road to Healing On- and Offline

253 **As Audre Lorde stated:** Audre Lorde, *A Burst of Light: And Other Essays* (New York: Ixia Press, 2017).

254 **In a think piece for *BuzzFeed*:** Niela Orr, "How 'Hot Girl Summer' Became Everyone's Favorite Meme Overnight," *Buzzfeed News*, July 24, 2019, https://www.buzzfeednews.com /article/nielaorr/hot-girl-summer-megan-thee-stallion.

255 **Black Girl Magic was popularized:** Julee Wilson, "The Meaning of #BlackGirlMagic, and How You Can Get Some of It," *HuffPost*, January 12, 2016, https://www.huffpost.com/entry /what-is-black-girl-magic-video_n_5694dad4e4b086bc1cd517f4.

256 **Diamond Sharp describes the movement:** Diamond Sharp, "Why Carefree Black Girls Are Here to Stay," *The Root*, August 9, 2014, https://www.theroot.com/why-carefree-black-girls-are -here-to-stay-1790876664.

260 **In a 2021 article for *Time*:** Kyra Aurelia Alessandrini, "Suicide among Black Girls Is a Mental Health Crisis Hiding in Plain Sight," *Time*, May 11, 2021, https://time.com/6046773/black -teenage-girls-suicide/.

261 **The suicide "epidemic":** Yanan Wang, "CDC Investigates Why So Many High School Students in Wealthy Palo Alto Have Committed Suicide," *Washington Post*, February 16, 2016, https://www.washingtonpost.com/news/morning-mix/wp/2016 /02/16/cdc-investigates-why-so-many-high-school -students-in-wealthy-palo-alto-have-committed-suicide/.

261 **According to a 2020 study:** Devin English et al., "Daily Multidimensional Racial Discrimination among Black U.S. American Adolescents," *Journal of Applied Developmental Psychology* 66 (January–February 2020): 101068, https:// www.sciencedirect.com/science/article/abs/pii/S0193397319 300462.

261 **Research proves that girls:** Jamie Ducharme, "Social Media Hurts Girls More Than Boys," *Time*, August 13, 2019, https:// time.com/5650266/social-media-girls-mental-health/.

262 **75 percent of victims of sexual assault experience:** Lynn Langton and Jennifer L. Truman, "Socio-emotional Impact of Violent Crime," Bureau of Justice Statistics, September 2014, https://bjs.ojp.gov/library/publications/socio-emotional -impact-violent-crime.

262 **To add to that:** Jameta Nicole Barlow, "Black Women, the Forgotten Survivors of Sexual Assault," *In the Public Interest*, February 2020, https://www.apa.org/pi/about/newsletter/2020 /02/black-women-sexual-assault.

262 **15 percent of Black female:** Asha Z. Ivey-Stephenson et al., "Suicidal Ideation and Behaviors among High School Students— Youth Risk Behavior Survey, United States, 2019," *Morbidity and Mortality Weekly Reports Supplements* 69, no. 1 (August 21,

2020): 47–55, https://www.cdc.gov/mmwr/volumes/69/su/su6901a6.htm.

262 **the actual suicide death rates:** Jagdish Khubchandani and James H. Price, "The Changing Characteristics of African-American Adolescent Suicides, 2001–2017," *Journal of Community Health* 44, no. 4 (August 2019): 756–763, https://pubmed.ncbi.nlm.nih.gov/31102116/.

263 **news report covering the tragedy:** Nigel Roberts, "Family Wants Answers after Girl with Autism, 10, Commits Suicide after Racial Bullying at School," BET, November 10, 2021, https://www.bet.com/article/67eiis/isabella-izzy-tichenor-suicide-utah.

264 **"increase in depression and suicides":** Luisa Bonifacio phone interview conducted with the author in November 2021.

264 **Given that Black therapists:** Luona Lin, Karen Stamm, and Peggy Christidis, "How Diverse Is the Psychology Workforce?," *Monitor on Psychology* 49, no. 2 (February 2018): 19, https://www.apa.org/monitor/2018/02/datapoint.

266 **social support has positive effects:** Emily A. Greenfield and Nadine F. Marks, "Sense of Community as a Protective Factor against Long-Term Psychological Effects of Childhood Violence," *Social Service Review* 84, no. 1 (129–147): March 1, 2010, https://www.ncbi.nlm.nih.gov/pmc/articles/PMC2865201/.

ABOUT THE AUTHOR

Brianna Holt is an author, screenwriter, and reporter living in New York City. Holt's writing has been published in *The New York Times*, *The Guardian*, *Rolling Stone*, *GQ*, *The Cut*, *The Atlantic*, Complex, and more, including her own column, Active Voice, through Medium's *GEN*. *In Our Shoes* is her first book.